D1204384

Authority Is Relational

The Library
St. Mary's College of Maryland
St. Mary's City, Maryland 20686

Authority Is Relational

Rethinking Educational Empowerment

CHARLES BINGHAM

STATE UNIVERSITY OF NEW YORK PRESS

Cover image, "Crowd Gazing," courtesy of Cathryn Bingham.

Published by
STATE UNIVERSITY OF NEW YORK PRESS, ALBANY

© 2008 State University of New York

All rights reserved

Printed in the United States of America

No part of this book may be used or reproduced in any manner whatsoever without written permission. No part of this book may be stored in a retrieval system or transmitted in any form or by any means including electronic, electrostatic, magnetic tape, mechanical, photocopying, recording, or otherwise without the prior permission in writing of the publisher.

For information, contact State University of New York Press, Albany, NY
www.sunypress.edu

Production by Kelli W. LeRoux
Marketing by Anne M. Valentine

Library of Congress Cataloging-in-Publication Data

Bingham, Charles, 1961–
    Authority is relational : rethinking educational empowerment / Charles Bingham.
        p. cm.
    Includes bibliographical references and index.
    ISBN 978-0-7914-7403-7 (hardcover : alk. paper)
    1. Education—Philosophy. 2. Authority. I. Title.

LA134.B56 2008
370.11'5—dc22   2007033900

                    10 9 8 7 6 5 4 3 2 1

Contents

Acknowledgments   vii

Introduction: Authority Is Relational   1

1. Texts and the Authority Relation   17

2. The Literary Relation of Authority   41

3. Relating to Authority Figures Who Are Not There   65

4. When Faced with Authority   87

5. Questioning Authority   111

6. Paulo Freire and Relational Authority   129

Notes   153

References   165

Index   169

Acknowledgments

My thanks go to Sasha Sidorkin, Donna Kerr, Cathryn Sedun, Stephen Haymes, and Claudia Ruitenberg, whose thoughtful conversation and insightful thinking have made this book possible.

The introductory chapter includes material reworked from "Authority Is Relational" in *No Authority Without Relations* (New York: Peter Lang, 2004). Chapter 1 includes a version of "I Am the Pages of the Text I Teach: Gadamer and Derrida on Teacher Authority," *Philosophy of Education*, 2001. Chapter 2 includes material reworked from "The Literary Life of Educational Authority," *Journal of Philosophy of Education*, Vol. 40, no. 3 (2006). Parts of chapter 3 appeared in a different version in "Language and Intersubjectivity: Recognizing the Other without Taking Over or Giving In," *Philosophy in the Contemporary World*, Vol. 6, nos. 3–4 (Fall–Winter 1999). Chapter 4 includes revised versions of the following essays: "Pragmatic Intersubjectivity, or, Just Using Teachers," *Philosophy of Education*, 2004; and, "Who Are the Philosophers of Education?" *Studies in Philosophy & Education*, Vol. 25, no. 1 (2005). Chapter 5 contains material first published in "The Hermeneutics of Educational Questioning," *Educational Philosophy and Theory*, Vol. 37, no. 4 (2005). Chapter 6 includes a version of "Paulo Freire's Debt to Psychoanalysis: Authority on the Side of Freedom," *Studies in Philosophy and Education*, Vol. 21, no. 6 (2002).

Introduction

Authority Is Relational

I have been a university professor for quite a few years now. I still can't let my students out of class early. I continue to keep them in class until the last scheduled minute, but that is not necessarily what I *want* to be doing. Why do I say that I "still" cannot let them out early? Because I hope to let them out early some day. I would truly like to let them out early, but I have an aversion to doing so.

It is not hard to pinpoint my aversion. It comes from the years prior to my role as a university professor, years during which I taught in high school and junior high school classrooms. My experience as a teacher during these early years was marked, as I assume many schoolteachers' experience has been, by an insistence on watching the clock, and by making every minute count. Authority figures at schools where I worked would insist on timeliness. Principals and assistant principals would remind us teachers to use every minute of class time. Messages such as, "Teachers, do not let your students into the halls until the bell has rung," could be heard daily over school loudspeakers.

In addition to being told to keep our students busy for every minute of each class, we were also told to keep ourselves busy until the last minute of the school day. We were warned, during faculty meetings, not to leave the school premises until the last school bell sounded. At one school where I worked, the windows of the principal's office looked out, strategically, onto the faculty parking lot. The principal could easily tell whose car was gone before three o'clock and whose was not. This principal would give the whole faculty stern warnings when the parking lot was beginning to look "too empty" at the end of the school day.

I once asked a colleague at my university if he has the same hesitance to letting students out of class early. To my surprise, he told me that he lets his students out of class early if the class discussion gets to a low

1

point. He said he considered the end of the class period not to be a set time; rather, class closure should reflect the pedagogical aims of the instructor. If learning has ceased, class time should be over. I on the other hand seem to have issues with time. It is clear to me that the authority structure in which I was apprenticed has gotten under my skin.

So I do still worry about classroom time "on task." But what interests me about these worries goes further. There is more to say than "this thing called authority has gotten under my skin." Indeed, the usual way of talking about authority is to say that authority is some "thing" to which we *succumb*. Yet, while my retentive tendencies are indeed a way of succumbing to intercom announcements and to the watchful eyes of principals, I find this simplistic understanding of my ingrained habits to be impoverished in many ways. While it might be true that one succumbs to authority, it is also true that authority operates in ways that need *not* be explained along the lines of domination and acquiescence to one who "has" this "thing" called authority. While it may be true that my current classroom practices *can* be seen as a matter of acquiescing to the authority of former administrators, it is also true that my current habits can be described in another way that is more fruitful. What interests me about my worries with time is the fact that these worries can also be understood as a matter of *relation*.

As a teacher, I seem to have gotten used to a certain *relation* to authority. I tend to relate to my students in the same way that I am used to relating to the authority figures I have answered to before. Authority, I would say, is not as much a matter of control (how my own authority figures have controlled me, how I control my students as an authority figure myself) as it is a matter of the relation that has been established between authority figures and myself, between me and my students. To break with past authority figures in this case would entail a certain defiance on my part, yes. But that defiance would not be simply "saying no to power." That defiance is more profoundly a willingness to change the sorts of *relations* that I am used to. To continue to be influenced by authority would be to continue with a relation that I have gotten used to. To act differently would be to change a relation to which I have become accustomed.

The aim of this book is to think about authority in terms of relation. It is my aim to look at scenarios of authority in ways that problematize, augment, and redefine prevalent notions of how authority works. For, current educational conceptions of authority assume that authority is primarily a thing that people have, a thing that is wielded by individuals who are in positions of power. Scholarly renditions and folk notions of authority alike thing-ify authority and describe it as a substance that is possessed by people in power who, in turn, use that thing, that authority, over others who are not in power.[1] Thus, it is common to hear statements such as, "That person has a lot of authority because she is a teacher," or, "Unfortunately I do not have much authority since I am only a student." Authority is usually construed as a possession to which one who lacks power either succumbs or does not succumb. In contrast, if we understand authority as a relation (as opposed to a thing), then an entirely new set of questions emerges. An entirely new sort of analysis is called for. Tired analyses of authority as a "thing" have outlived their usefulness.

CURRENT CONCEPTIONS OF AUTHORITY AS SUBSTANCE: THE PROGRESSIVE, THE TRADITIONAL, THE CRITICAL

Take, for example, recent scholarly debate about educational authority. Such debate over authority usually ends up in an impasse precisely because it treats authority as such a "thing." On one hand, progressivists hold that authority is best dealt with by giving it up.[2] In progressive camps of educational thought, it is assumed that authority is harmful to the student. It is thought that the more authority a teacher has, the less chance the student will have to gain autonomy or agency. In the context of progressive education, one hears such things as, "How can we share authority with our students?" "How can we try not to be authority figures in classrooms?" and "She is a very personable teacher; she really doesn't flaunt her authority."

The traditional argument, on the other hand, holds that authority must be embraced. Traditionalists contend that authority is a moral good that comes when one acquires knowledge and institutional responsibility. Following this line of thought, a teacher is a beneficent authority figure because of what she knows, because of her classroom role in loco parentis. The traditional argument asks us to recognize that some folks are in a position to help others.[3] Can authority be wrong if it is employed in a thoughtful manner? Authority, following this traditionalist logic, is completely acceptable as long as one uses one's authority to help those who are not in authority. By using one's authority, one can cultivate the capacities of those who are themselves not yet authority figures.

Against the backdrop of a progressive rejection of authority and the traditional acceptance, the critical argument maintains that authority *must* be used, but only for the purposes of teaching for social justice.[4] The critical argument suggests a qualified use of authority. It is qualified in that it does not embrace authority per se, but embraces only the authority of those who speak for social justice. So unlike the traditional perspective that advocates the practical necessity of the various versions of educational authority (personal, institutional, scientific, cultural, etc.), the critical perspective encourages only those versions of authority that promote freedom and social change. And unlike progressive perspectives, the critical perspective does not assume that the use of authority is somehow *naturally* at odds with social justice. The critical argument advocates the use of authority when teaching for human freedom is at stake.

Progressives argue against authority. Traditionalists embrace it. Criticalists embrace it at certain times. Granted, these are stereotyped positions that I have laid out, it is certainly true that these positions tend to treat authority as a "thing." These three positions consider authority to be a sort of zero-sum commodity. It is said that the more authority one person has, the less another person has, that authority is a substance to be rejected or embraced, a thing that is either bad or good. I am not saying that these three positions do not offer important insights into the use and abuse of authority. Certainly, each of these positions makes some sense in their respective rejection, embrace, and qualified embrace of authority *as substance*. Yet, when these positions are taken, I am struck by the extent to which each is hamstrung by the assumptions they make about the thing-ified nature of authority. Certainly, if authority were a thing, then I would have to agree with the critical perspective. Yet, it is my contention that authority is in fact not a thing. It is a relation.

Let me say it again: These three positions, as well as most prevalent explanations of authority, make a fairly primitive ontological presumption regarding authority. They presume that authority is a thing. According to these sorts of explanations, the same mistake is made that a folk-meteorologist might make if he or she were to assume that wind is itself a substance. To be sure, one can take the position that wind is a substance in and of itself. And to the extent that one takes that position, it might even make sense to wonder if more wind is a good or bad thing. It might make sense to wonder if we should try to stop the wind on certain occasions, or if we should try to increase the wind on other occasions. Yet, from a more sophisticated, more accurate position, one should understand that wind is in fact a movement of air. It is a movement of air that exists in relation to the differing temperatures of various land masses and bodies of water. It exists in relation to differences in atmospheric pressures. The wind exists only in relation to other circumstances. With a more sophisticated understanding of the wind, there is no meteorological sense in the endeavor to create more wind, or to create less wind. There is only sense in asking how the wind acts in relation to different events.

It is the same with authority. The common sorts of arguments either embracing or decrying authority fail to deal with the most important of all questions concerning authority, namely: How does authority work *in relation*? So I propose that we think about educational authority in a way that is uncommon at present. I propose that we consider how educational authority operates. For while progressivists argue against it, while traditionalists embrace it, and while criticalists warn about using it judiciously—while these various perspectives on the 'substance' are being articulated, none of them look deeply into the question of *How?* To ask the question *How?* is a different matter altogether than arguing for or against. To ask *How?* is to look for models that illustrate the workings of authority as relation. In the chapters that follow, I examine a few such models.

Let me offer another example. This one was told to me by one of my university students. A university sophomore, let's call her Julie, told the following story in class. Julie is at school to become a teacher. And, as a student who will soon be a teacher, she pays close attention to her own relationships vis-à-vis teachers so that she might learn from them habits that would benefit her own teaching. She told this story to illustrate the ways in which some university professors are sympathetic to the genuine experiences of students while some are not.

Julie had just encountered a traumatic experience. Her grandmother had passed away. She had been very close to her grandmother when she was a child, though she was separated now from her by quite a distance, having moved out of state to attend university. Julie spent a week away from school to attend the funeral and to be with her family in this time of mourning. And, as it so happened, she did not inform her professors about her absence until after she returned to school, until she was once again in attendance at the courses where she had been absent.

Julie was quite apprehensive before returning to her classes. She did not want to be seen as making excuses for the coursework she had missed, and she felt a bit guilty for not contacting her instructors earlier. But at the same time she wanted to let her professors know that she had been absent for a very legitimate reason, for an event that was much more significant than any week's worth of lectures.

On the first day of her return, she approached her English professor after class. She told the professor the reason she did not attend the previous week's classes. The professor acted in a very sympathetic manner. She did not say a word to Julie about the absence itself, not a word about Julie's classwork. Rather, she asked if Julie had been close to her grandmother, to which Julie said yes. Julie told her of how they used to play card games together in her childhood. The professor also asked if Julie needed anything in order to get through this rough time. Julie and her English professor stood at the front of an empty classroom: "If there is anything I can do for you," the professor said, "please let me know." Julie thanked her for her kind words.

Julie contrasts this first reception to a different sort that she faced upon explaining her absence to her history professor. As in the previous class, Julie told her history professor about her absence.

The history professor said this: "Well, you know that you missed last week's quiz don't you?"

"Yes," Julie responded.

"Well, you're going to have to make that up within two days."

"Alright," Julie said.

"And," her professor said, "I'll need to have a written verification of your absence. I'll need that note before you can actually take the make-up quiz. That's my policy for every student no matter how extenuating the circumstances."

Julie responded that she would do so. But as she recounted this story to me, she added a couple of details about what went through her mind as this incident unfolded. Julie explained: "As my history teacher was talking, I became so angry with her for ignoring my feelings, for being so unsympathetic. She lost all credibility in my view. After that, I refused to work hard in that class. She lost her authority as a teacher over me."

What intrigues me about this story is a bit different than what intrigued Julie. While Julie was intrigued by the different affective relationships that were established by these two professors, I am more interested in the small detail that Julie included about the way she treated the professor who was so unsympathetic to the tragic experience she had gone through. For, as Julie explained, her instructor's callousness caused her to discount her authority from that time forward. I am interested in this discounting because it points to an aspect of educational authority that is so often overlooked, the aspect of relation. Educational authority is generally treated as a monologic rather than a dialogic experience. It is rarely investigated with an eye to its enactment as a circuit.

Julie's small detail is significant because it goes against so much educational thought. The bulk of educational thought assumes that authority is located solely in the hands of instructors. That is to say, it assumes that Julie is not a key player in the workings of authority, and that her sort of small detail is just that, small and insignificant. I contend, though, that Julie *is* a key player in the relation of authority. Because authority is a relation, there is not just one person who "has" authority and one who does not. Rather, each person is involved. Both Julie *and* her professor are involved in the relation of authority. It is my contention in this book that Julie's experience must be listened to. Her experience shows us that there is a certain circuitry to authority. Authority gets enacted in circuits where each participant has a role to play, where authority is not simply a monological enactment, where it takes the participation of at least two people for authority to gain purchase. It works as a circuit instead of working unidirectionally or monologically.

CONCEPTIONS OF AUTHORITY AS NONRELATIONAL: MONOLOGICAL AUTHORITY

I have mentioned current conceptions that treat authority as a substance rather than as a relation—the progressive, the traditional, and the critical conceptions. Indeed, one way to construe authority as something other than relation is to treat authority as a substance that is possessed by people. However, this understanding of authority as substance is closely related to another assumption that is made about authority: that authority is monological. To assume that authority is a thing is first to assume that it stands alone in spite of human relations. But oftentimes, there is an accompanying assumption that authority is held and applied by one person only, that it is monological. In spite of the fact that experiences such as Julie's happen all the time, an unquestioningly monological understanding of authority has dominated, and continues to dominate, many educational and noneducational accounts.

Such a monological view of authority can be traced back at least as far as its Kantian inheritance. Indeed, as evidenced in his pivotal article of 1784, entitled "What Is Enlightenment?" Immanuel Kant shows that the entire project of Western Enlightenment is grounded in a monological understanding of authority. In this article, Kant encourages his readers to have the courage *not* to rely on the authority of others. As he notes,

> Enlightenment is man's emergence from his self-imposed imma-
> turity. Immaturity is the inability to use one's understanding
> without guidance from another. This immaturity is self-imposed
> when its cause lies not in lack of understanding, but in lack of
> resolve and courage to use it without guidance from another.
> *Sapere Aude!* [dare to know] "Have courage to use your own
> understanding!"—that is the motto of enlightenment.[5]

According to Kant, then, authority comes at individuals from above, from the unilateral direction of one who has authority *toward* one who has none. In Kant's analysis of authority, it is up to the individual to either submit to such authority, or, to have the courage to be "mature" by using one's own reason. One must fight the authority of others by using the authority of one's own reason. In this Kantian formulation of Enlightenment, there is no mention that authority is in any way affected by the individual's reaction to that authority. Authority may be directed at one person from another, it may be directed from an institution or tradition toward a person. But, authority remains monological in the Kantian tradition. For Kant, the best (the most "mature") way to deal with authority is to ignore it and to use one's own authority instead. Kant thus sets up a zero-sum game of authority the likes of which I have described in the context of progressive, traditional, and critical approaches to educational authority. Kant's conception of authority depends on a thing-ification of authority. And in addition, it assumes that authority works through an atomistic, monological relation between those "in" authority and those who are "faced with" authority.

In more recent educational thought, too, authority continues to be treated as a monologic entity. Interestingly, the monologic account of authority continues in full force even for thinkers who are otherwise thoroughly dialogic in their orientation to education! For example, monologic authority makes a particularly interesting appearance Paulo Freire's seminal work, *Pedagogy of the Oppressed.*[6] This appearance is interesting given the fact that Freire is otherwise so successful at advocating a relational form of pedagogy. For Freire, authority is virulently monologic even at a time when there is to be reciprocity in the teacher/student relation. In Freire's dialogic education,

> The teacher is no longer merely the-one-who-teachers, but one who is himself taught in dialogue with the students, who in turn while being taught also teach. They become jointly responsible for a process in which all grow. In this process, arguments based on "authority" are no longer valid; in order to function, authority must be on the side of freedom, not against it.[7]

Even as Freire advocates an education that scissors back and forth between teacher and student, authority itself remains a one-sided possession of individuals who are free.

It is actually the work of Freire that has made me the most attuned to the deeply entrenched, indeed the seemingly irrational, insistence that authority needs to be understood as monologic. His work has made me realize how important it is to rediscribe authority in a relational way. Why the work of Freire? Because he protests too much. His proclamation that arguments over authority will disappear in dialogic education is just a little bit too neat. His proclamation that authority simply jumps over to the side of freedom is in fact a very obvious crack in his own well-formulated methodology, and it performs the following unfortunate maneuver: (1) Monologic education is full of authority.

(2) Authority in such a monologic education is wrong. (3) Dialogic education must replace monologic education. (4) Since dialogic education promotes freedom, authority will switch to the side of education that promotes freedom. It is as if authority is just one of those monological things that will change for the better when educational actors engage with each other in a dialogic way.

Interestingly, Freire supposes that authority remains monological, remains on one side, even when educational interactions become dialogic. He supposes that authority works monologically *against* freedom when it is oppressive, and monologically *for* freedom when it is liberatory. For Freire, the object of dialogic education is to change the nature of authority from freedom-crushing to freedom-enhancing, even while authority remains essentially monologic. In contrast to Freire, I contend that authority is always already dialogical in nature. Freire's understanding of authority is steeped in the Enlightenment tradition inaugurated by Kant even while his vision of the human person is intersubjective in ways that Kant could not have endorsed. Freire does not entertain the possibility that there could be dialogic authority. Indeed, dialogic experiences with authority such as Julie's are pushed aside even by such a dialogic educator as Freire.

SPEAKERS AND LISTENERS

At a very basic level, even during a simple exchange of words between two people, authority gets enacted in relational ways. When a person speaks, I listen. What happens when I listen? The relation of authority begins. When I listen to another, I partake in authority. I partake as I halt my own speech long enough for the other to speak. When I listen, the other does not listen but speaks instead. I listen, the other speaks. Through my listening, I enact a relation of authority. Through the other's speaking, she enacts authority as well. Authority is not a "thing" lying in wait. It is not first "possessed" by the speaker, then "used." Authority does not happen until we, the listener and speaker, enter a relation.

When I listen, I partake in the relation of authority. When another speaks, she partakes also. Neither of us "has" authority. Neither of us "succumbs" to authority. Rather, we create the relation of authority within the speaking and within the listening. The relation of authority would be incomplete without listener. It would be incomplete without the speaker. To speak to no one is to be outside of authority. To listen to no one is to be outside of authority. Authority is not present until the speaker is listened to. It is not present until the listener is spoken to. Authority comes to exist when the relation is made. Until the relation is made, authority is not yet present.

An important example of the authority relation between speaker and listener can be found in Louis Althusser's *Ideological State Apparatuses*.[8] Althusser describes the experience of a person who is hailed by a policeman on the street, a person who is *talked to* by another who is in authority. When such a hailing takes place, it is not simply the policeman who enacts authority. Indeed, the role of the person being hailed is just as central to the enactment of authority as the role of the policeman. For what is interesting about this sort of hailing is that the policeman might be calling to *anyone* on the street when he calls out, "Hey, you there." Yet, in spite of the fact that he might be calling on just anyone, the hailing takes effect when the one who is being hailed responds by acknowledging that the anyone is *he* rather than someone else. Althusser narrates this event as follows:

> There are individuals walking along. Somewhere (usually behind them) the hail rings out: "Hey, you there!" One individual (nine times out of ten it is the right one) turns round, believing/suspecting/knowing that it is for him, i.e. recognizing that "it really is he" who is meant by the hailing. But in reality these things happen without any succession. The existence of ideology and the hailing or interpellation of individuals as subjects are one and the same thing.[9]

While Althusser focuses on the ideology at work, I want to focus on the authority at work. In this example, the police man is a figure of authority. The person on the street has his back to the policeman. He does not even know for sure that the policeman is a policeman. He does not even know for sure that it is *he* who is being hailed by the policeman. Yet in spite of all of this ambiguity, the man turns around because he assumes that it is he who is being hailed. When he does turn around, he becomes "interpellated" into (quite literally, "called into") the position of being named as "you" by the policeman. Importantly, the authority of the policeman is not a preexisting authority. It is clearly not preexisting since the policeman's authority qua policeman is not known until after the man has turned around, until after the man has himself participated in the relation of authority.

Any authority that the policeman might have over the man who believes he is being called cannot have been in existence before the turn of the man. For, before that turn, it is not at all clear that it is *this* man over whom the policeman has authority. It is the turn itself that establishes the policeman's authority per se, and it is the turn itself that establishes that the policeman "has" authority over this particular man. It is in fact the man's participation in the relation of authority that establishes both the existence of the policeman's authority and its direction (being ultimately directed at the man by virtue of the man's turn toward it). As I have stated above, it is the listening and the acceptance of the relation itself that establishes authority. The authority was not actually present until a relation has been established between speaker and listener.

Franz Fanon provides another excellent example of the authority relation between a listener and a speaker, this time in the context of a racist colonial regime. In *Black Skins/White Masks*, Fanon describes a black man's reaction to the call of a white boy on the streets of Paris. Fanon recalls being hailed as a black man by a white boy:

> [A boy calls out] "Dirty Nigger!" Or simply, "Look, a Negro!"
> I came into the world imbued with the will to find a meaning in things, my spirit filled with the desire to attain to the source of the world, and then I found that I was an object in the midst of other objects.
> Sealed into that crushing objecthood, I turned beseechingly to others. . . . I was indignant; I demanded an explanation. Nothing happened. I burst apart. Now the fragments have been put together again by *another self*.[10]

The boy may have hailed him by saying, "Dirty nigger," or he may have hailed him by saying simply, "Look, a Negro." Whatever the case, being hailed as a black man on the streets of a racist white regime causes the black man to listen, to be entered into a racist relation with white authority. As Fanon recounts this incident, he reminds us how devastating such an encounter can be for a black man. In a racist world, being called out as a black man, either viciously or as a simple matter of fact, is a threat and a derogation.

Fanon reminds us that in a racist world it really doesn't matter whether the words used to hail are "dirty nigger" or simply "hey you." Whatever the case, the black man's hearing of the white boy's hail creates a relation of authority between the white boy and the black man that is devastating in its psychological import. Certainly the white boy "has" little authority before he does the hailing. Perhaps just as certainly, the white boy "has" little or no authority even after the hailing. It is not that one (white) person has authority and the other (black) person has none. It is rather that a relation of racist authority is established as soon as one (white) person speaks and another (black) person listens.

In a racist world, racist authority is not enacted until a relation is established. That is not to say that racist authority is somehow less odious or less oppressive because it exists in relation rather than as some sort of preexisting "thing" or "substance." Emphatically and viciously, racist authority diminishes the agency and freedom of those who are marked as people of color in a racist world. It does so through relation. Indeed racist authority obtains its particular viciousness *because* it is relational. Racist authority is not something abstract: It establishes real hierarchies and concrete instances of domination between real people who have flesh-and-blood relationships.

If these two examples described by Althusser and Fanon seem extreme, then let me go back to a simpler example of listening and speaking. This example comes from an exchange that can be heard every day in thousands of classrooms across the world. It happens when roll is taken on the first day of class. On the first day of class, a teacher looks at her roll sheet and calls out, "Deborah Williams?" At the sounding of her name, Deborah answers, "Here." Before the calling, Deborah is a name on a piece of paper. She is a faceless place-marker, a student-to-be, a name whose person might well be a mistake on the classroom roster. The name might well stand for an absence that might never be present in class. Before the answering, the authority of the teacher over this Deborah Williams is hypothetical at best. Before the answering, Deborah has every opportunity to opt out of her role as student vis-à-vis this teacher. Before the answering, Deborah may decide that she does not like the teacher's manner. She may decide to absent herself from this particular class by standing up and telling the teacher that she is in the wrong class. She may not reveal that she is indeed assigned to be a student in this class. It is only through the answering of Deborah that authority becomes enacted between the teacher and herself.

AGENCY AND RELATIONAL ANALYSIS

Once again, I want to emphasize that authority gets enacted whenever one person speaks and another person listens. But what's more, I would even say that authority gets enacted *whenever there is a relation* between two or more people. Just as there is no way to avoid the enactment of authority once one has gained the ear of another, so, too, is there no way to avoid the enactment of authority once two or more people have entered into a relation with each other. As soon as there is a relation between human beings, there is authority. That is to say, relation is a *sufficient* condition for the existence of authority. As well, the enactment of authority does not happen until there is a relation between two or more people. That is to say, relation is also a *necessary* condition for the existence of authority. While it may seem surprising that the commonplace, even benign, experiences of listening and speaking are sufficient events for the enactment of authority to happen, I want to go much farther: authority is enacted whenever there is relation among people, no matter how benign or commonplace the relation is.

To realize that authority is enacted even during those seemingly benign moments when one person speaks and another person listens, to realize moreover that authority is enacted whenever there is a relation between people—to realize these matters puts us on a very different course of analysis with regard to authority. First of all, an analysis that looks at authority as relational must stop asking the same tired questions about authority that have been asked for so many centuries under so many guises. Those tired questions are, Is authority a good thing or a bad thing? Must we embrace authority or dismiss authority? Should authority figures give over their authority or cling to it? Certainly, these tired questions have been asked with good intent. From Immanuel Kant, to Paulo Freire, to progressive, traditional, and critical theorists, these sorts of questions have been asked in order to figure out how to deal with authority. They have been asked in order to figure out how to increase freedom and agency when human beings are faced with authority.

Yet, when authority is understood as relation, then a different sort of analysis is required. Authority, like the wind that we encounter when we walk outside, is not something that will go away. It is not something that can be avoided. Authority as relation is not to be eschewed or embraced per se. Rather, it must be analyzed on its own terms of reference. Does this mean that we must abandon the Enlightenment search for freedom and agency when it comes to authority? Absolutely not. It simply means looking elsewhere than to the tired questions that have been asked for so long to so little avail. Indeed, in the chapters that follow, I will be concerned precisely with questions of human freedom and human agency. Yet, these questions will be pursued on the assumption that authority takes place in relation rather than on the side of one person who clearly "has" authority in his possession.

To begin looking at the theoretical work that helps to unpack the relational life of authority, let me borrow from Michel Foucault's analysis of power. Foucault reminds us that power is *productive* in nature. For Foucault, power is not only a restraining force that works against people. It is not only a force that people need to break down in order to gain more freedom. Power is also constitutive. It constitutes people's freedom at the same time that it constrains their freedom. Power may sometimes be oppressive, but it also makes a double gesture: it often insinuates itself into the very pleasures that it serves to repress. In this way, power cannot said to be primarily repressive. It is both repressive and active in the lives of individuals who are enabled by power at the same time that they are constrained by it. Power "doesn't only weigh on us as a force that says no," but it also "traverses and produces things, it induces pleasure, forms knowledge, produces discourse."[11] For Foucault, then, it can never be a question of "saying no" or "saying yes" to power. Even in the "saying no" or "saying yes" power is already at work.

Foucault also points out that, when it comes to power, the most important thing we can do is to separate power from capacity.[12] That is to say, we must analyze power in a way that does not assume that agency and freedom are always at odds with power. In fact, because power both constitutes and constrains, human capacity cannot be the same as power. Sometimes, human capacity will be decreased by power but sometimes it will be increased by power. There is not a simple either/or binary when it comes to taking a stand vis-à-vis power. Power does not *either* constrain *or* enhance human capacity. Thus, Foucault encourages us to separate power from capacity in order that we might analyze power in a thorough manner without prejudicing our analysis by assuming that power is only that which diminishes human capacity. If we presume, beforehand, that power is that-which-diminishes-human-capacity, then our analysis of power will be hamstrung by such a presumption.

Foucault's insights into power ring true for authority. Authority, because it is a relation, works on all sides of human interaction. Authority produces as well as constrains. Let me go back to my own example of being reticent to let students out early. A relational understanding of authority will entertain the possibility that authority was working with me as well as working against me. Authority affects classroom practices in two senses. It affects them in the sense that it changes them, yes; but it also affects them in the sense that it puts them into use. For example, using the entire class period has become a working part of how I understand pedagogy in my own classroom. Using the entire class period changes the ways I plan lessons. It gives rise to affective investments about the quality of education I provide. (I am actually *proud* that I use the entire class period.) The *entire* block of classroom time is a platform upon which my pedagogical sensibilities find a certain orientation. The authority that constrains my options also gives meaning of my options.

So, it is important for any relational analysis of authority to follow Foucault in his advice to separate capacity from power. In my own analysis, I too want to separate capacity from authority. When people engage in a relation of authority (and as I have been arguing, all relations are relations of authority), we must be able to distinguish between the types of authority relations that enhance capacity from those that diminish capacity. It is not true, as most Enlightenment conceptions of authority would have it, that human agency is automatically diminished when there is a relation of authority. Sometimes relations of authority will be dominating, but sometimes such relations will be agentive. What we should stay away from is the assumption that capacity is linked in fixed, non-agentive ways to the exercise of authority. It is most important to determine those instances when human capacity can be enhanced even as the relation of authority is being enacted. Authority relations can lead to domination and submission, *or* they can lead to reciprocity and agency. Indeed, as the following chapters will show, I am concerned with detailing the ways that authority relations can lead to human agency even when authority itself is as unavoidable as the wind that blows.

I have said that all relation entails authority and that all authority entails relation. Of course, such a claim sounds immense. Such a claim is indeed immense. It is too immense for the educational analysis that I want to carry out in this book. In the chapters that follow, I will be concerned with some very specific instances of the authority relation that one encounters in educational circumstances. I will be concerned, in chapter 1, with the textual relation of authority. Chapter 2 will consider how authority relations must be understood as literary and linguistic. Then in chapter 3, I will look into the educational authority that gets enacted when teachers (as authority figures) are not present, are not in the same room, with the students they have been teaching. In chapter 4, I will look into the ways that students can use the authority relation to their own advantage, the ways that students can "use" teachers. In that chapter, I will return to the work of Michel Foucault (among others) as part of an elaboration on the ways that students can use authority to enhance capacity and agency. Chapter 5 will be concerned with the ways that authority gets enacted through the process of questioning and answering in education. And finally, chapter 6 will explore the matter of relational authority in the context of the critical pedagogy of Paulo Freire. In the end, this book does not attempt to make a grand statement that solves all questions about educational authority. It is an attempt to look at a few, and only a few, of the salient practices in education where relational authority is at stake. It is an attempt to isolate a few instances of educational authority and to show ways in which such instances can lead to human agency especially on the part of students.

CHAPTER 1

Texts and the
Authority Relation

Recently, I began one of my university courses in a way that was for me unusual. I told the students that one of the books we were going to read was new to me, that I had never read it before. I justified my choice of the book, and the fact that I had not read it yet, by mentioning that it had come highly recommended by two colleagues whom I respected very much and who had read it in manuscript form. And it was a brand new book, I told my students, hot off the press. Thus, I thought it reasonable that we read the book together. We would learn from each other.

Actually, what was unusual for me was that I *told* my students this. I had, when teaching a course, read texts with my students, for the first time, quite a few times. But I had never prefaced a course by admitting that we would do so.

The students seemed to take the admission in stride, until the day we discussed the book. One student, let's call him Darrel, was visibly upset with the book. His classroom comments were highly critical of the text. And while he spent some time in class offering judicious and well-argued critiques of the book, it seemed as if he was biding his time, holding back. Darrel finally burst out, "You know, I promised myself I wasn't going to say this, but I don't think this book has anything to offer to teachers, to schools, or to anyone concerned with education. This book has nothing to offer educators, Dr. B!"

This sort of critique is not what was remarkable, though. Many other students critique texts that I have chosen. They are encouraged to do so and should do so. What surprised me happened about a week later when I was talking with Darrel in the hallway. Going out of his way to explain his outburst in the previous week's class, Darrel said that he still did not think the book was useful for educators. "But what bothered me even more," he said, "was that you had not even read the book before you assigned it. That's what got to me."

What struck me about Darrel's comment was mainly that I had never had my own authority as a professor positioned in quite this way, between flattery and condemnation, between all-knowing and unknowing, between progressive and traditional, between one who learns along with his students and one who lets them learn something wrong, between the 782 books on the shelves of my office that I had read and this one that I *hadn't* read. Given these encounters with Darrel, both in class and out, I am sure that my own teaching authority was in play, but I was not quite sure how.

In this chapter, I want to examine the authority relation and the place of texts therein. Why look first to texts? Because it is important to start examining the relation of educational authority not in general, but with an eye toward the context in which such authority gets enacted. In education, this context is, quite literally, a *con*-text, a "with text." The text is an integral part of the educational relation of authority. For, authority comes in many forms: familial authority, legal authority, religious authority, institutional authority, state authority... Yet, not all of these noneducational forms of authority include a use of the written word. I examine here the place of texts in the authority relation because texts are an inevitable component of *educational* authority. When authority gets enacted in education, it is most often through the use of texts.

Indeed, as I will put forth in this chapter, the text enters the relation of education authority in some complicated ways. For, texts are not only *used* as part of this relation. In addition, texts become an integral part of the relation itself. Students and teachers engage with texts and these texts become, to a greater or lesser extent, a part of them. In this regard, it is worthwhile to note another etymological link: The very word, *authority*, has its history in matters of *author*-ship. Who writes what, and who reads what, are central to authority, and especially central to educational authority. It is thus very important to look at the place of the book deep within relations of educational authority. The place of the book in the relation of educational authority is not a distant one. Students and teachers are intertwined with the book when authority gets enacted. The relation of authority in education makes us readers and authors. It ties us in organic ways to the text. Authority in education is thus not only a relation between people who use texts; it is also a relation between people who are in the process of becoming, themselves, textual. To partake in educational authority is to partake in authorship.

To think about the place of the book, this chapter will outline two theoretical frameworks for interpreting the textual nature of authority: one based on the hermeneutics of Hans-Georg Gadamer and one based Jacques Derrida's logic of the "supplement."[1] By outlining these two frameworks, I try to shed some light on the complicated link between teaching authority and the text. I find that the works of both Gadamer and Derrida are vital in teasing out the messy relationship between the learner, the teacher, and the book. It is this messy relationship that I believe my student Darrel was pointing out. For Gadamer, the authority of the text is separate from, and preferable to, the authority of the teacher. Gadamer sees a difference between textual authority and human authority. He sees the former as more beneficial and the latter as less beneficial. However, Derrida sees more of an organic link between the two. I therefore use Derrida's logic of the supplement to extend the Gadamerian analysis. Derrida reminds us that we are an actual part of the texts we teach.

As well, this chapter will examine a work of literature that helps to further elucidate the place of texts within the authority relation. I will examine the play, *My Country! My Africa!*, written by Athol Fugard and set in South Africa during the Apartheid regime.[2] Fugard's play offers a powerful lens for further analysis of the central, yet complicated, role that texts play within relations of educational authority. His play reminds us that texts bear not only on the relation between a student and his or her teacher, but also on larger social movements where authority is at stake, social movements such as the anti-Apartheid struggle in South Africa.

GADAMER ON AUTHORITATIVENESS
VERSUS AUTHORITARIANISM

Gadamer's analysis of teaching authority is based on his more general understanding of hermeneutic authority. So I begin with synopsis of hermeneutic authority as described by Gadamer. Hermeneutic authority, as a part of the to-and-fro interchange between text and interpreter, derives from the cultural "horizon" upon which a text rests in order to make sense to the reader, in order to lay claim on the reader. According to Gadamer, the authority of a given text rests in its ability to be understood within a set of cultural and historical cues that are available for understanding not only because they wait to be discovered within the closed pages of the text, but also because they draw upon a tradition of understanding that is to some extent already shared with the reader or interpreter of the text. (Such a tradition may be shared either consciously or unconsciously.) For Gadamer, authority is thus not merely a way of describing the quality of the knowledge or theory or narrative that a text imparts. Authority is also a description of the extent to which a book participates in a conversation whose language the reader is familiar with. Following Gadamer, a book is authoritative to the extent that it is informative and to the extent to which it lends itself to a cultural and historical understanding that takes place between the reader and the book.

That is not to say that authority works only in positive ways, however. As Gadamer points out, there are certainly times when authority contributes to rigid thinking, when it promulgates prejudices. He notes,

> If the prestige of authority displaces one's own judgment, then authority is in fact a source of prejudices. But this does not preclude its [authority's] being a source of truth, and that is what the Enlightenment failed to see when it denigrated authority.[3]

Authority is certainly in a position to restrict freedom, but it is also in a position to let freedom run its course by allowing a conversation to take place. In his later work, Gadamer gives names to two different kinds of authority, the sort that is restrictive and the sort that is productive. He points out that if a person is "authoritarian," then he or she draws upon institutional power and hierarchical position in order to demonstrate authority. For Gadamer, this sort is restrictive. But he also points out that if one is "authoritative," then one draws upon superior knowledge and insight, upon cultural traditions that allow conversations to take place instead of shutting them down.

"The word 'authoritative,'" writes Gadamer,

> precisely does not refer to a power which is based on authority. It refers, rather, to a form of validity which is genuinely recognized, and not one which is merely asserted. . . . Anyone who has to invoke authority in the first place, whether it be the father within the family or the teacher in the classroom, possesses none.[4]

Authoritativeness is a quality that depends upon learning and knowledge, upon texts and shared cultural understandings. Authoritativeness, unlike authoritarianism, is a productive version of authority. And, following this distinction, a teacher should be authoritative, but should not be authoritarian. An authoritative teacher, like a text that "speaks" with authority, can lay claim to a wide array of knowledge, draws upon a wide cultural horizon that serves as backdrop for a conversation in which curriculum becomes intelligible to students.

What is significant here is precisely the link that Gadamer makes between teaching and authoritativeness. He points out that teaching authority can be construed from a hermeneutic viewpoint, from an appeal to the cultural and historical horizons that make understanding available in the first place. Critiquing the Enlightenment's "subjection of authority to reason," Gadamer asks us to reconsider the possibility that teaching authority is not necessarily a bad thing, and that a student's being made subject to teaching authority is not necessarily a loss of freedom.[5] Yes, it is oppressive if one exercises authority over another by virtue of institutional position. Yes, the Enlightenment tendency to eschew authority is valid when the authority of church or state or school impinges on one in a way that is a threat to personal autonomy or the use of reason. However, Gadamer points out that there are elements of authority that are useful and empowering as well. Just as the authority of a text derives in part from a larger cultural horizon that actually makes the text intelligible to begin with, so too, for Gadamer, teaching authority derives in part from a shared set of understandings. He argues that the cultural and historical background that supports teaching authority is empowering rather than hindering as it contributes to the growth of others rather than curtailing their freedom.

What I find interesting about Gadamer's hermeneutic understanding of authority is that it points to the territory that is at stake in my student's comments. Gadamer's analysis suggests that teaching authority, if it is to be empowering instead of hindering, should be based upon the knowledge of the teacher, that teaching authority is shored up by the books the teacher has read. Following Gadamer, one can envision the authoritativeness so vividly depicted in many professors' offices today: all of the books behind the professor's desk, those books that she has read with such care, serve to shore up authority in a legitimate way. Looked at in this way, the book that I did not read before the course started is missing from the shelf. My authoritativeness is weakened and illegitimate to the extent that I had not read the text long before.

Gadamer's analysis of authority distinguishes "genuine" authority from nongenuine authority by separating the knowledge-based-ness of authoritativeness from the power-based-ness of authoritarianism. If we were to follow Gadamer here, we would conclude that knowing the text backward and forward and keeping one's aims "genuine" vis-à-vis students (aiming to impart knowledge rather than aiming to manipulate) is the basis of valid teacher authority. Along these lines it is perfectly reasonable to suggest that the professor acts authoritatively by assuming full responsibility for the book, for *reading* the book before it appears on the syllabus, for taking authoritative (as opposed to authoritarian) responsibility for the book. Being authoritative by knowing the book well is a primary responsibility the professor has for his or her students. *Not* reading the book beforehand, but assigning it nevertheless, Gadamer's analysis implies, the professor practices authoritarianism; the professor relies on her institutional position, not on her firsthand knowledge of the work, to convince the student to read that text. This is the sort of authoritarianism that Darrel had every right to question.

As I see it, though, Gadamer's analysis of teaching authority stops short of being able to provide a more nuanced understanding of Darrel's complaint. While Darrel's complaint makes a lot of sense when set against Gadamer's distinction between authoritativeness and authoritarianism, his complaint also points to the limitations of the way in which Gadamer applies his own hermeneutic project to the matter of teaching authority. For when Gadamer speaks of the two types of teaching authority, he creates an either/or scenario that forces an instructor into a corner: either he has genuine knowledge, or he employs institutional power. In this way, Gadamer's thinking on teacher authority contradicts the much more nuanced thinking of his overall hermeneutic project. While Gadamer's overall project is concerned with the incredibly complex interpretive relationship between people and texts, his thinking on teacher authority ghettoizes the teacher/text relationship into a matter of good and bad authority.

Teacher authority should not be split into the two categories of authoritativeness and authoritarianism and then left at that. Such dichotomizing forces an explanation of Darrel's complaint that is too simplistic. What is needed is a way to push farther into the teacher's relation to the text in order to see if Darrel's complaint might be something other than a complaint about authoritarianism. In other words, there is a need to push Gadamer's educational thinking along.

I AM THE MISSING PAGES OF THE TEXT I TEACH

Jacques Derrida, with his notion of the "supplement," opens an important brief on this question of how teaching authority relates to the text. In a very straightforward sense, the teacher can be construed as a supplement to the text, as a welcome addition that makes the text itself more intelligible to the student. This understanding of the instructor-as-supplement follows a long tradition of educational thought that calls upon the teacher to clarify curriculum for students, to make texts more available to their understanding. It's important to think more thoroughly about this role of the instructor as supplement, and that can be done with the more complex notion of supplementarity that Derrida introduces, especially in *Of Grammatology*.[6]

As Derrida points out, the straightforward understanding of supplementarity is limited. The supplement must not be construed solely as something that is *in addition* to a given text. The process of supplementarity entails a double gesture that must be thought in its doubleness. The supplement to a text must be construed both as something that adds to that text *and* as something that makes that text whole, that both augments and completes.

For Derrida, remembering this doubleness of supplementary is absolutely essential. To forget the supplement's doubleness is to practice a forgetfulness of textual complexity. To begin with, a textual supplement enriches a text by bringing it more fully into the light of day, into the realm of human understanding, into presence. Noting this first role of the supplement, Derrida writes,

> The supplement adds itself, it is a surplus, a plenitude enriching another plenitude, the *fullest measure* of presence. It cumulates and accumulates presence. It is thus that art, *techne*, image, convention, etc., come as supplements to nature and are rich with this entire cumulating function.[7]

But also, the supplement instills itself as a *natural* part of that which it supplements. We might think here of a person who takes a vitamin supplement. The vitamin supplement is an addition, yes, but it stands in for a *natural* lack. It becomes a *natural* part of the body. So for Derrida,

> the supplement supplements. It adds only to replace. It intervenes or insinuates itself *in-the-place-of*; if it fills, it is as if one fills a void. If it represents and makes an image, it is by the anterior default of a presence.[8]

More than a merely an add-on by which a presence such as a text is made more present, the supplement also instills itself as a necessary part of the text. The supplement represents the text, yes, but in doing so it also becomes part of the text's economy, part of its very health.

One way to begin considering the link between supplementarity and pedagogy is to remember that teachers are in a relation to their texts that to some extent parallels the complicated relationship between the spoken and the written word. Teachers are often called upon to relate or facilitate the written word by spoken means. This oral/written distinction has connections with Derrida's project. For Derrida, the logic

of supplementarity follows from his critique of philosophers who prioritize either the spoken or the written word. Long-standing paradigms of
linguistics such as Rousseau's or Hegel's or Saussure's have tended to
prioritize either the spoken or the written pole of the speaking/writing
binary. Speaking is taken to be either the ideal form of writing or its
messy human counterpart. The written word is often considered to be
merely a conduit for the spoken or, conversely, what is spoken is often
considered to be merely a conduit for the written word.

But, as Derrida points out, language theory has been unwilling to
think about the ways that writing actually infects the spoken work and,
vice versa, the ways in which spoken word continues to infect language.
There is no way to cleanly separate the spoken from the written because
neither of them works *simply* as a conduit for the other. The spoken
word has a written-ness that can no longer be left out of consideration;
the written word has a spoken-ness that will not go away. To put it very
simply, the word *period* now has an ordinary meaning based on its
grammatical function ("I am done with this book, period!") and the
word "ain't" *is* now in the dictionary. Both the period (".") and "ain't"
have become supplementary. This cross-infection of the spoken/written
has ramifications for the teacher/text relationship.

While the above is a general (and admittedly cursory) description
of supplementarity, it is interesting, and germane to this discussion of
my student's concern, that Derrida links his notion of supplementarity
more explicitly to pedagogy in his analysis of Rousseau's *Emile*. For
Derrida, pedagogy is fundamentally grounded in a tradition of
supplementarity, in a tradition of putting the instructor in place of a
parent, of supplementing parental teachings. Reading *Emile*, Derrida
notes that pedagogy functions within an economy where "it is indeed
culture or cultivation [supplied by the instructor] that must supplement
a deficient nature, a deficiency" that cannot be adequately supplied by
the parent.[9] Quoting Rousseau, Derrida goes on to say that "[a]ll orga-
nization of, and all the time spent in, education will be regulated by this
necessary evil: 'supply [suppleer] . . . [what] . . . is lacking' and to replace Nature."[10] Pedagogy is an endeavor caught up in the logic of
supplementarity: children need to be given their supplements not only
because they lack a certain amount of knowledge, but also because such
knowledge completes them and becomes inseparable from them. Education is both *an addition to* and *a natural part of* childhood; the
instructor's role is an addition to the parent's and is itself parental; the
classroom both contributes to certain habits of nature and creates a
naturalness out of certain habits.

This Derridian discussion of supplementarity is not as far from
Darrel's concern as it might seem. What is striking and provocative in

Darrel's comment is that there is a logic of supplementarity that works alongside of or, to stay with Derrida's theme, seems to supplement, such a straightforward discussion of authority as Gadamer's. For while there is a sense in which pedagogical authority must depend upon the instructor's grounding in textual knowledge, in what Gadamer names the "genuine knowledge" of the "traditionary text," there is also a sense in which the instructor and the text stand within an economy of supplementarity that makes the instructor both *an addition to* the text and *an integral part of* the text. Following Derrida's logic of supplementarity, Darrel's experience of lack when he discovered that the book had not been read by me is not only a matter of disgust with the teacher's lack of authoritativeness. It is also a reminder that the book is somehow incomplete without the instructor's presence. The book experiences the teacher not only as an extension of itself, but as a supplement that it cannot do without. Like the teacher whose introduction of culture into the "natural" family life of the child becomes part and parcel of that "natural" family life, the instructor whose job it is to supplement the text also becomes part and parcel of the very text whose message she attempts to convey. When I complain that my teacher has not read the book, I am not only complaining that she is not authoritative enough; I am complaining also that the book is missing some pages.

Comparing Gadamer's description of "authoritativeness" to Derrida's understanding of "supplementarity" is instructive. While both versions link up with Darrel's concern about the relation of the book to teacher authority, this comparison points out how Gadamer relies on a one-way understanding of authoritativeness that is limiting. For Gadamer, the movement of text and textual tradition runs from historical tradition, through texts, then out to the mouth and fingers of the instructor. The instructor is a conduit for the message of tradition and for the message of the text. That is not to say the text of the tradition must be conservative or regressive; only that the movement is from what has been previously known to what the student is to learn. The pedagogical problem, as I see it, with Gadamer's understanding of authority is not that it depends upon tradition in any regressive sense. Indeed, the textual authority upon which I build my syllabus, and upon which I speak, may be based on progressive or even radical education. The problem with this understanding of authority is that it depends upon a pedagogical movement that is one-way.

In contrast, Derrida's logic of the supplement highlights the two-way movement that complicates the teacher's position with respect to the text. The teacher participates in more than a one-way trajectory from tradition to text to teacher to student. She is also a complicatedly *real* part of the text that he teaches. Teachers and students are in a relation with their texts. When I teach subject matter, I am not only a representative of, nor only an addition to, the tradition from which I have constructed my syllabus; I am also an active part of that tradition. I act as a spokesperson of the book that I may or may not have read, but I also push the book this way or that way as if I am one of its chapters. This supplementary understanding of the teacher's role vis-à-vis the text suggests that Darrel's critique was more than a claim that I wasn't properly prepared to teach the text, more than a claim that I was not authoritative enough; it was also a claim that the text itself was somehow lacking a part of itself without which it would fail to be whole. Because the supplement is both an addition to, and a part of; because of this, my disconnection from that text threatened the authority of the book itself. My *not*-reading was a weakening of the book.

BEING CONTENT

So I consider it important to follow Derrida's logic of supplementarity when it comes to the complicated connection between teacher and texts. I have been inspired by Darrel's challenge. It was a challenge that I assumed initially to be a questioning of my authority, but that I now see as a questioning of the authority relation between me and the book that I hadn't read. I think it is too easy for educators to think along one-way lines when it comes to curriculum, authority, and pedagogy. It is too easy for educators to assume, like Gadamer, that pedagogical authority is primarily a matter of deploying one's knowledge of curriculum in a judicious manner. Following Derrida's lead, we must also think about the relation of pedagogical authority vis-à-vis the text. Because, as the instructor, I am part of the educational text, it follows that, in spite of the way I teach, I nevertheless have an active role in constructing the way educational texts are read by my students. Assuming that Derrida has a (supplementary) point, it is impossible for a student to read a classroom text without, in some way, reading me. Thus, the habits that students form around reading curriculum are going to reflect, at least in part, the habits they form around reading *me*.

To make this notion of "reading the instructor" more specific, imagine that I am a white man and that I have chosen to read Toni Morrison's *Playing in the Dark* with my class.[11] (To summarize inadequately, Morrison's text is an analysis of how the white racist imagination that has come to structure canonical literary works in the United States.) Having assigned this text, the problem of teacher authority rests not only on whether I have understood the text deeply enough, on whether I can refrain from *forcing* the text on my students. It refers also to how I, as a white man, become part of the text's own analysis.

Morrison's text, as complicated as this may seem, becomes in my class a text that is co-authored in black and white, by Morrison and me. To become educated about Morrison's argument means, at least in my class, also to become educated about how a white man can be in relation to that argument.

When I teach Morrison's text, and when I do so with the logic of the supplement in mind, I must be cognizant of the perlocutionary (to borrow John Austin's term) effects that I put into play as a white man who teaches that text.[12] Being part of that text, I will also be part of the ways in which my students read that text now and in the future. As part of that text, my whiteness will be a barrier for some students and an invitation for others. Importantly, I cannot shirk that barrier status, or that invitational status. That status will not go away by laying the onus of learning on my students nor will it go away by presenting the text as if I am merely a conduit through which my students reach text directly. The white perspective that I bring to this text on white racism will be part of the lesson that this text teaches. And conversely, if my teaching strategy is to act as if I do not have a perspective on this text, then the message this text sends may very well be that a white person has no pages to add to Morrison's text. Whatever I say—even if I say nothing—speaks pages about a white understanding of the racist imagination.

To return to the objections raised by Darrel, I now have a deeper respect for the validity of his reaction. It now seems to me that there are at least two distinct reasons for his response. On one hand, it may have been that Darrel was reacting to what he thought of as a particularly authoritarian act on my part. Here I am following Gadamer: because authority becomes authoritarian when not based on genuine knowledge, it is entirely justified to accuse an instructor of resorting to authoritarianism when he chooses texts based not on knowledge, but upon his institutional position. Following a Gadamerian logic, my choosing of that text can justifiably be criticized because it depended more on my institutional power to set curriculum than it did upon my genuine knowledge of the text. On the other hand, Darrel may have been reacting to the textual incompleteness that my admission revealed. Here I am following Derrida: because the instructor resides in a position of supplementarity vis-à-vis her text, curriculum is simply not complete unless it is supplemented by the instructor's own authoritative voice. Pedagogical authority can be described as the authority that books borrow from teachers. Because I had not read the book before I assigned it, the *text's* authority became permanently marred in this student's eyes. Along with Derrida, a case can be made that Darrel knew the text he had purchased was missing some pages.

SUPPLEMENTARITY AGAINST THE BACKDROP
OF PREDOMINANT PEDAGOGIES

One way or another, both of these versions of textual authority (the authoritative and the supplemental) show how the book supplements the teacher. On the one hand, we have a picture of a teacher who enacts authority because he or she has the ability to draw upon the authority of the book. Drawing upon the authority of the book rather than drawing upon the authority of one's position as teacher, is, at least according to this first version, a helpful way to enact authority. In this first picture, we find that the teacher has a choice to make between the extrinsic and the intrinsic. Either she can put in play the external authority of the institution to which she belongs, or, she can enact the internal authority that comes with the book's knowledge. In this first picture, there is a difference in distance between the illegitimate, institutional authority that one might enact and the legitimate, textual authority that one might enact. One is far away, while the other is close. It is in this way that the authoritarian person draws on an authority that is distant while the authoritative person enacts authority that is close. The judicious enactment of authority deals with knowledge that is close at hand, with a text that is sutured in tight.

On the other hand, we have a picture of a teacher who stands in a certain relation with the text that she teaches. In this picture, there is also something that is far away and something that is close. This something is the *same* thing. It is the book. When one thinks of the teacher as a spokesperson for the book, as a voice for the written text, then the book seems far away from the teacher. The spokesperson can stand at a great distance because she is merely an echo of what the book says. She is like the stereo speaker that can stand at a great distance from wherever the recording itself is being played. When, however, one thinks of the teacher as a spokesperson who is part and parcel of the book's presentation, then the teacher and the book turn out to be located at the same place. When the spoken word is taken to be central to the written word, then the teacher is closely bound to the text that is being taught.

Indeed, a lot of educational theory about authority hinges on the sort of relation that exists between teachers and texts. In the introductory chapter, I gave a brief overview of three different orientations toward educational authority: the progressive, the traditional, and the critical. I described the progressive orientation as a complete dismissal of authority, the traditional orientation as an embracing of authority, and the critical orientation as a pragmatic embracing of authority, an embracing that endorses authority as long as that authority serves liberatory purposes. Actually, each of these three orientations also includes an orientation toward the relation that exists between teachers and texts. Let me explain.

The progressive orientation toward educational authority assumes that texts need little support from teachers. Progressives assume for the most part that texts can stand on their own, can speak for themselves. Thus, in classrooms inspired by progressive pedagogy one often finds a rather hands-off approach to the content matter of the texts being learned. In such classrooms it is most often assumed that the text is better learned if it is kept separate from the instructor, if it is dealt with by the student, for the student, rather than by the teacher, for the student. To give one small example, I need only recall the responses that I have received from progressive educators when they have listened to me tell my story about Darrel. I am not exaggerating when I say that most of my *progressive* colleagues who have listened to my story have doubted whether Darrel's complaint was legitimate. Those colleagues who call themselves progressive have, for the most part, few qualms about teaching a book that one has not already read. After all, from the progressive perspective, it is not the teacher's role to offer direct instruction on a text's content. To put this in terms of the teacher's relation to the text: the progressive teacher keeps his or her distance from the texts that are being learned. The progressive orientation sees the relation between teacher and text as a distant one.

If the progressive orientation construes the relation between teacher and text as a distant one, the traditional orientation is just the opposite. For traditionalists, it is just fine for teachers to teach the content matter of a book. After all, the use of authority for such a benign purpose— that of teaching texts—is perfectly acceptable. Indeed, because students seem to benefit from the direct use of pedagogical authority by the teacher, the use of such authority is more than acceptable; it is pedagogically necessary. It is necessary in that it aids in the learning of texts. And because of this pedagogical necessity, traditionalist theory carries with it a perspective on the proximity of teacher to text. Because of the necessity of pedagogical intervention on the part of the teacher, the traditional teacher is a *confrere* of the text. The teacher keeps the text close at hand.

As one might expect, the critical perspective blends the progressive and the traditional. From the viewpoint of the criticalist, the ultimate aim of education is to foster a healthy distance between text and teacher. The steady-state at which a critically educated student eventually arrives is one where the student no longer depends upon the authority of the teacher to shore up her own knowledge of the text. However, from the critical perspective, the student may not be able to arrive at such a steady-state on her own. Why? Because hegemonic ideology prevents the student from reading texts properly. While the criticalist might want to keep her distance from the text, while she might hold such a distance as an ideal, she knows that, in fact, hegemonic ideology requires her to intervene in the student's reading of the text. If students are to read texts on their own, as in the progressive tradition, they might not be able to see past the implicit ideology of those texts. Hence the necessity of an enlightened, critical educator who can help students to see past ideology and into the "true" message of the text. As one might expect, the criticalist is a mixture of progressive distance from the text and traditionalist proximity. She tries to be distant from the text, but is willing to be close to the text when such proximity is required in order to debunk hegemonic ideology.

Once again, I have stereotyped these three positions—the progressive, the traditional, and the critical—unreasonably. I have done so for heuristic purposes. Indeed, these stereotypes are not far off the sorts of general orientations that guide many a thoughtful teacher. By explicating these three ways that educational authority gets positioned vis-à-vis the text, I have wanted to show the various ways that texts enter into the relation of educational authority. Texts are part and parcel of the authority relation. Depending upon how one theorizes the authority relation, depending upon the orientation that one takes toward pedagogy, texts can be construed as either more central or less central to that relation.

TEXTUAL AUTHORITY AND RELATION

Actually, I would say that each of these positions gets it all wrong. A text is not to be distanced from the teacher because one is progressive, held tight because one is conservative, nor held tight strategically because one is a criticalist. In contrast, I would take up Derrida's position, namely, that texts *always* supplement the one who teaches. In contrast to the orientation of these three popular positions, the teacher is always part and parcel of the text that is being taught—even if he or she has not read the text! A mistake is made by the progressive, traditional, and critical orientations alike. Their mistake is twofold. First, these orientations assume that one's relation to a text is somehow voluntary, that it is based upon the will of the teacher, upon either the unwillingness of the teacher to teach the text through direct instruction, or upon his willingness to do so. On the contrary, the will of the teacher has very little to do with the teacher's textual authority. Teachers supplement texts whether or not they *want* to do so, as the story of Darrel so clearly illustrates. Teachers are always already close to their texts, but this has nothing to do with some traditionalist orientation that advocates direct instruction based on the teacher's knowledge of the text. Teachers are always already close to their texts because the pedagogical relation of authority is thoroughly textual.

Second, these orientations are off the mark because they see the text as a matter of monological authority (coming from the teacher) rather than as part of a *relation* of authority. As is the case when progressive, traditional, and critical educators treat authority as a substance, when these folks theorize the place of the book, they do so solely from a teacher-sided perspective. That is to say, these perspectives assume that it is the distance or proximity of the teacher to the text that is paramount. They assume that the decision of the teacher to stay close (in the case of traditional and critical orientations) to the book, or the decision of the teacher to stay far (in the case of progressive orientations) from the book, is primarily the teacher's. Following these three conceptions of the textual life of authority, it is the teacher's stance vis-à-vis the text that is paramount. The student is hardly involved.

Yet in contrast to this picture of a teacher who has monological authority over the educational life of the text, let's remember Darrel (and for that matter Julie, too). Darrel is intimately involved in the way his instructor gets positioned in relation to the text. Far from being the passive recipient of the teacher's textual orientation, students (and not only Darrel, but all students) are integral to the ways in which teachers get configured as supplements. As I have argued above, teachers are supplemental to texts whether or not they choose to be, whether or not they disavow their role as textual authorities. It is precisely because of the fact that students construe their teachers as textual authorities that teachers become supplemental to their texts. In this way, the textual authority of teachers is relational: students impute textual authority to teachers whether teachers "want" that authority or not.

DISCOUNTED SUPPLEMENTARITY

In this section I would like to further illustrate the textual relation by looking more closely at instances when students discount the teacher and the text. One of the problems with discussions of educational authority, a problem that I tried to articulate in rehearsing the "common" assumptions held about authority, is that they tend to focus too narrowly on the teacher side of the educational relation. Such discussions tend to be monological. Indeed, when I examined my own interaction with Darrel and the supplemental position it put me in vis-à-vis an educational text, I still focused too narrowly on the ties between teacher and book. Surely, this teacher/book tie means something to the student as well. If the teacher is tied to the book, how does this bear on the one who is receiving the education? What circumstances lead a student to break with supplemental authority? When is supplementarity an intrusive aspect of the authority relation rather than a benign one? What are the political dimensions of the tying-together of the teacher and the book? How can student resistance be understood in light of such tying?

To further explore this matter, I turn to Athol Fugard's play *My Children! My Africa!*[13] Fugard's play is set in the fascist South African regime during the Apartheid era. It explores the relationship between two high school students and one of their teachers. Thami, a black South African student and Isabel, a white South African student of Afrikaaner descent, attend different high schools. They come into contact, though, because each has been chosen to take part in a literary competition, a competition that tests their respective knowledges of English literature.

Mr. M is their coach. He is a black South African and is a teacher of English at Thami's school. Although he is a black South African teaching in an all-black school, he helps to coach an extracurricular literary competition in which the teams are comprised of both blacks and whites. Thus, although Thami is Mr. M's student in an all-black school while Isabel attends an all-white school, Mr. M coaches both Thami and Isabel after school hours as they prepare together for the competition. Isabel ventures into a black neighborhood where she has never been before in order to take advantage of Mr. M's coaching.

The play is set in the late 1980s when there is considerable student resistance, in schools and on the streets, against the Apartheid government. It is this militant anti-Apartheid unrest that serves as a political backdrop for the play. Although the play starts out during a time when students are attending school regularly, as the play progresses, students have begun to show their resistance by boycotting the black high school where Thami attends and where Mr. M teaches. They are refusing to attend school in order to force reform in the Apartheid system. By the end of the play, Mr. M, being himself opposed to the boycott, gives names of some of the boycotting students to the police. Mr. M, the teacher, becomes Mr. M the informer. He is denounced as such by the boycotting students. Toward the end of the play, he is killed by an angry mob because of his status as an informer. This happens in spite of Thami's efforts to make a public apology in his name. Let this suffice as an introduction to the play. In what follows, I want to use some of the words of the characters in this play to investigate the relation between students and textual authority.

To get at this relation, let us first examine the textual authority of the teacher in Fugard's play, Mr. M. In particular we can look at the way he stands as a supplement in relation to the English literature that he teaches and that forms the basis for his coaching of Thami and

Isabel. As the play unfolds, we learn about Mr. M's unwavering love of the texts he teaches. In the terms I have presented in this book, we learn that he has become part and parcel of the texts he teaches. He and they have entered a supplemental relation. For example, as play proceeds Mr. M reveals to us that his entry into the teaching profession is marked not only by a desire to teach young people, but more importantly by a desire to supplement the experiences of his own life with the experiences that he reads about in books. He has decided to enter the teaching profession because he believes that a lifelong apprenticeship to books will serve him better than any other sort of career might do. He decides to follow a career of teaching because he believes that a career of reading will, in fact, change him for good.

Mr. M's decision to take up a career of books is described as follows. I quote at length Fugard's beautiful rendering of this decision:

> This was my home, my life, my one and only ambition . . . to be a good teacher!. . . . That ambition goes back to when [I] was just a skinny little ten-year-old pissing on a small gray bush at the top of the Wapasberg Pass. . . .
>
> I went to the teacher who was with us and asked him: "Teacher, where will I come to if I start walking that way?" . . . and I pointed. He laughed. "Little man," he said, "that way is north. If you start walking that way and just keep walking, and your legs don't give in, you will see all of Africa! Yes, Africa little man! You will see the great rivers of the continent: the Vaal, the Zambesi, the Limpopo, the Congo and then the mighty Nile. You will see the mountains: the Drakensberg, Kilimanjaro, Kenya and the Ruwenzori. And you will meet all our brothers: the little Pygmies of the forests, the proud Masai, the Watusi . . . tallest of the tall and the Kikuyu standing on one leg like herons in a point waiting for a frog." "Has teacher seen all that?" I asked. "No," he said. "Then how does teacher know it's there?" "Because it is all in the books and I have read the books and if you work hard in school little man, you can do the same without worrying about your legs giving in."
>
> He was right Thami. *I* have seen it. It is all there in the books just as he said it was and I have made it mine.[14]

In this moving passage, Mr. M tells of the ways that books have become part of his very life. By choosing teaching as a career, he has had the chance to go on the very same journeys of the mind that his former teacher had been able to go on. Importantly, his choice to become a teacher was made precisely because being a teacher would require a rigorous assimilation of books. He knew early on that becoming engrossed in books would change his life, that such a textual profession would take him places both literally and metaphorically. Mr. M is indeed a dedicated teacher. He follows through with this teacherly ambition to let books change his life. Having been a teacher for decades, he is now able to say, in a very supplementary way, "It is all there in the books just as he said it was and I have made it mine."[15] Mr. M has let the teacherly reading of books supplement his life experience. He and the books he has read are now intertwined.

The books that Mr. M has read also supplement his life experience in a particularly political way. During this time of political upheaval and student resistance in the South African townships, he has clung to the notion that learning itself will set the stage for political change in a way that no other political activities will be able to do. He maintains that the words used by those in the South African freedom movement are very weak compared to the articulate political phrases that a well-educated person can construct. Says Mr. M:

> Slogans don't need much in the way of grammar do they. . . . [*Picks up his dictionary. The stone in one hand, the book in the other*] You know something interesting, Thami . . . if you put these two on a scale I think you would find that they weighed just about the same. But in this hand I am holding the whole English language. This . . . [*the stone*] is just *one* word in that language. It's true! All that wonderful poetry that you and Isabel tried to cram into your beautiful heads . . . in here![16]

Weighing the stone and the dictionary together, Mr. M demonstrates that even his political strategies are supplemented by, are shaped by, the books that he values so much. His strategy for changing the South African political system is tied to the books that he has taught, and learned from, over the course of his teaching. For Mr. M, these books, and the articulate language they represent, are linked not only to his authority as a teacher but to the authority that he claims to have about how politics should be conducted. The educational authority of Mr. M's texts has gotten under his skin even when it comes to politics.

Mr. M's relation to his texts is quintessentially "traditional" if the traditional orientation toward texts can be said to entail a fairly blind faith that canonical texts carry the moral weight to change things for the better in this world. It is also a traditional orientation in the sense that this teacher assumes it to be his role to pass down the wisdom of these canonical texts, to "stay close" to his texts as I have described earlier. Indeed, Mr. M has good reason to stay close to his texts. He has been a successful teacher who has "seen" the great rivers and mountains of Africa, who has made them his own as a result of the texts to which he has been devoted. This experience alone is proof enough, at least for Mr. M, that texts carry a moral weight to change people's lives for the better. And, when it comes to political change, Mr. M's belief in the power of texts seems to have borne fruit as well. For, by coaching Thami and Isabel, a black student and a white student, together, Mr. M has successfully caused the color line of Apartheid to be crossed. His coaching of Thami and Isabel, and their surprising friendship in spite of Apartheid laws, proves Mr. M's position: that social change can be effected when people of different races use literary texts as a common ground for gathering.

At least at the personal level, and in one small instance of the political arena, it must be admitted that Mr. M and his texts have, together, created the circumstances for moral change in the world. They have enriched Mr. M's life and they have enabled a subversive engagement between a black and a white student to occur in spite of a fascist Apartheid regime. With the aid of Mr. M and his favorites—Coleridge, Wordsworth, Byron, Keats, Arnold, Shelley—Thami and Isabel forge a close friendship during a time when their paths might otherwise not cross at all. It might be said, from the two versions of textual authority that we looked at earlier, that Mr. M has been admirably authoritative (rather than authoritarian) and that the educational texts he has been involved with have been a true supplement to his life. Mr. M holds a traditional reverence for his texts, one that keeps texts close at hand. And, his supplementary relation to his texts has benefited both himself and his students.

LESSONS FROM ATHOL FUGARD

However, from the perspective of Thami, Mr. M's prize student, the supplementary relationship between teacher and text looks quite different. Indeed, Fugard's entire play hinges upon Thami's *relation* to Mr. M's text-driven authority. For, Thami's relation to Mr. M's text-driven authority cannot be extricated from the authority of the great number young black students (and young black *former* students who have already quit school), people who, like Thami, want a different version of authority than Mr. M has in mind. Thami does not have a straightforward respect for the textual authority of his teacher. Thami knows that Mr. M's textual authority does not have power to change society. He knows that Mr. M's moral stance is in conflict with the political action needed to change a country steeped in racist laws. Mr. M himself describes this conflict:

> Respect for authority, right authority, is deeply ingrained in
> the African soul. It's all I've got when I stand there in Number One [his classroom]. Respect for my authority is my only
> teaching aid. If I ever lost it those young people will abandon
> their desks and take to the streets.[17]

Thami is one of those young people who will take to the streets.

From Thami's perspective, the authority of Mr. M does not stand alone; it stands in competition with the authority of those students who decide to take to the streets. From Thami's perspective, there is a choice to make about *which* authority he will enter into a relation with. As the play progresses, Thami's political place in the anti-Apartheid struggle becomes more firmly affixed "to the streets." Mr. M's literary knowledge, his supplementary relation to the texts he teaches, is discarded by Thami in favor of more pressing political commitments. Speaking of Mr. M, Thami says that "[h]is ideas about change are the old-fashioned ones. And what have they achieved? Nothing. We are worse off now than we ever were. The people don't want to listen to his kind of talk anymore."[18] In Thami's eyes, the "old fashioned" quality of his teacher's authority undermines its more positive potential. Thami is faced with the textual authority of his teacher and the political authority of his comrades. He chooses to authorize the latter rather than the former. This, in spite of the benevolent, textual authority of Mr. M, authority which, as we have seen, does change lives for the better, at least on some small scale.

Let us draw a few insights from Fugard's play. First, the relation of the student to the authority of the teacher/text does not only depend upon the sincerity of a teacher's engagement with the text. Indeed, Mr. M is sincere to the core about his teaching, about his love for literature, about the potential for literature to actually *create* experience and opportunity. Mr. M has concrete experience from his own life that literature can make one's life more worth living. Because of his own life experience, he assumes that he can change his student's life for the better in the same way. He is sure of this fact:

> He is my favorite. Thami Mbikwana! Yes, I have waited a
> long time for him. To tell you the truth I had given up all
> hope of him ever coming along. Any teacher who takes his
> calling seriously dreams about that one special pupil, that
> one eager and gifted young head into which he can pour all

that he knows and loves and who will justify all the years of
frustration in the classroom.[19]

Mr. M hopes to "point to Thami and say: And now ladies and gentle-
men, a full university scholarship if you please."[20]

Truly, Mr. M's "textual sincerity" fills this drama with pathos. Mr.
M is a tragic figure whose tragic flaw is his devotion to the written
word. His devotion is especially tragic because he assumes that his
"best" student will necessarily follow him in his textual footsteps. Mr.
M makes the same assumption that so many good-intentioned, well-
read teachers make. He assumes that if his authority is enacted in a
sincere way, with the right texts, then his "best" students are sure to
benefit. He believes this so much that he is willing to become an informer against his students' political activities with the hope that his
students will go back to the classroom and learn what he has to teach
them. He loses his life by clinging to these good intentions. His good
intentions with respect to his texts have little bearing on the efficacy of
the authority relation that is enacted between him and his students.

A second insight to draw from Fugard's play is one that I have
briefly touched upon in the introductory chapter. It is that educational
authority works in circuits. And, the student has an active (rather than
a passive) role in this *circuit* of authority. Yes, Thami is the prize student of Mr. M, the student Mr. M hopes to influence the most through
his great love for the written word. Yet at the same time, Thami is also
the student who has the most ability to either authorize of de-authorize
Mr. M's teaching. Thami's status as Mr. M's "best" student not only
signifies that Mr. M's hopes are pinned on Thami. It also signifies that
the very authority Mr. M so cherishes, the authority of the canon, or
the written word—this very authority depends upon Thami's own authorization for it to be enacted. When Thami decides that Mr. M's ways
are too old-fashioned, when he decides to authorize the actions of his
comrades rather than the books of his teacher, then the textual authority that Mr. M would like to enact falls flat. In spite of Mr. M's sincere
engagement with his texts, and in spite of his belief that book learning
is the only way to prevent students from taking to the streets, Thami
takes to the streets anyway.

Fugard's play teaches this general lesson about the authority relation between students and teachers and texts: Authority works in a
circuit from teacher to student and from student to teacher. It works
through a circuit of *authorization*. It is not the case that the teacher is
the only one to enact authority. Authority does not start from the
teacher and then go toward the student. Rather, authority is borne out
of an authorizing circuit that gets established between the teacher, and

the student, and the text. For authority to be enacted, it is not enough for there to be a show of textual authority on the side of the teacher. It is not enough for the teacher to know her books through and through. It is not enough for the teacher to act in authoritarian ways. It is not enough for her to have good authoritative intentions. The teacher always needs to be authorized by the student just as much as she needs to enact authority. Indeed, we might even say that authority has not been initiated by the teacher until it has been authorized by students. This concept of circuitry is central for understanding how textual authority gets configured from a student's perspective, and it is central for a more general analysis of authority's relationality. To say it again: authority works in a circuit. The authority of one person comes into being because it is authorized by another person. This notion of circuitry will be especially important later on when we look into the authority of questioning and when I offer an extension of Paulo Freire's conception of authority.

A final insight to draw from Fugard's play takes us back to Derrida's notion of the supplement. The insight is this: from the perspective of a student, sometimes texts can become *too* supplemental to the teacher. I have mentioned that Mr. M's tragic flaw stems from his extreme devotion to the canon and in his extreme belief that book-learning will change both his own life and the lives of his students for the better. That is from Mr. M's perspective. From Thami's perspective, Mr. M's supplemental relationship to his texts looks a bit different. As we saw above, Thami thinks that his teacher's "ideas about change are the old-fashioned ones. And what have they achieved? Nothing. We are worse off now than we ever were. The people don't want to listen to his kind of talk anymore."[21] Interestingly, Mr. M is being understood by Thami differently than he might want to have himself understood. Somehow, the "old-fashioned" books that Mr. M reads get linked in Thami's mind (and in the minds of those who have Thami's ear) to "old-fashioned" ways of acquiescing to Apartheid laws, which in turn get linked to "old-fashioned" ways of teaching and learning. I do not think that Mr. M means to be "old-fashioned" in the derogatory sense that the students have in mind. Mr. M surely wants to change the Apartheid regime. After all, he facilitates the color-line crossing friendship of Thami and Isabel.

Yet notwithstanding Mr. M's intentions, he has become indelibly marked as old-fashioned by Thami and his comrades. From the perspective of Thami, he has become "hyper-supplemented." Mr. M stands as a dramatic metaphor for the many teachers who become so inexorably branded by students with such labels as "the old-fashioned English teacher," or "the Darwinian science teacher," or "the jock physical education teacher," or "the laissez faire education professor." While Mr.

M's status as symbol of an old order is surely more rich and complicated than the simplistic labeling of a teacher who teaches a certain
subject matter, what I want to stress here is the way in which such
labeling must be taken seriously as it effects the ways students authorize
and de-authorize teachers. Mr. M is de-authorized because he is per-
ceived as "hyper-supplemented" and inflexible. Thinking back to the
example of Julie that I offered in the previous chapter, we could say that
she de-authorized her history professor in much the same way. That is,
once she found out that his only concern was for his own curriculum,
once she found out that he was so hyper-supplemented as not to see
that her grief was a significant pedagogical concern, then she de-
authorized both him and the history he wanted to teach her. From the
perspective of a student, one's authority is not always shored up by
proximity to one's subject matter.

This chapter has tried to pay attention to the place of curriculum
in the educational relation of authority. If the introductory chapter was
a general outline of how we might think of educational authority in
terms of relation, this chapter examined an inevitable component of
that relation—the written word. To restate the point that I have been
building to: the relation of authority can be understood at a textual
level. Teachers are supplementary to texts in a Derridean sense. Because
we are supplementary to texts, we cannot disavow our role as textual
authorities. When students read texts, their teachers are inevitably involved. Whether teachers take an active role in interpreting texts for
students, or whether teachers take a passive role by trying to let students interpret texts for themselves, students nevertheless authorize teachers to be part and parcel of the curriculum. Educators cannot escape
this fact no matter how progressive we might aim to be. Because authority in education is primarily a textual relation, teachers and students are in relation to texts just as much as they are relation to each
other. In the next chapter, I will go one step farther by asking, "What
sort of relation is this, this relation of authority?" As I will show in the
chapter that follows, the relation of authority is a literary relation.

CHAPTER 2

The Literary Relation
of Authority

If authority is a relation, what is this relation like? In this chapter, I will make the case that the authority relation is like a literary relation. To consider how one relates to authority in education, it is best to consider how one interprets literature. With this in mind, I will retell a short story by Franz Kafka. I will use Kafka's story, and Jacques Derrida's interpretation of that story, to show the authority/literature connection. Also in this chapter, I will examine how we must change the ways we currently conceive of communication. By doing so, I will extend the brief remarks made in the introductory chapter about the authority that gets enacted when people speak and listen to each other. As I will show, current, "thingified" conceptions of authority are hamstrung by the "sender-receiver" model of communication. I suggest that we reconceptualize communication itself as a matter of interpretation. Doing so, we can once again foreground the fact that authority is a relation. It is a relation through and through, even in its speaking and listening.

EDUCATIONAL AUTHORITY IN KAFKA:
FORCE WITHOUT SIGNIFICANCE

In Franz Kafka's tale, *Before the Law*, a man from the country approaches a building where a doorkeeper is standing watch.[1] In front of the building, the man asks if he might be allowed inside in order to meet "the Law" that resides therein. The doorkeeper tells the man that he cannot admit the man at the moment, but it is possible that the man

41

will be allowed to enter later. The door to the law is open during this inquiry, but when the countryman tries to peer through, he is met with laughs by the doorkeeper. The man is dismayed: "The Law, he thinks, should be accessible to every man and at all times."[2] The man is told that there are more doors inside and more doorkeepers even more powerful than this one. The man from the country is relentless, though. He waits for days and years. He gives gifts to the doorkeeper on occasion but to no avail. Finally, the man grows old and approaches death, still waiting to be let in to the law. At the end of his life he asks why there has been no one else who has joined him, during all those years, to seek admittance to the law. To this, the doorkeeper answers that "this door was intended only for you. I am now going to shut it."[3]

The short stories and novels of Franz Kafka, having introduced into the English language the term *Kafkaesque*, are famous for the enervating, paralytic mood they evoke. Kafka's narratives generally present the struggles of a protagonist who is faced with a pressing condition, but the protagonist generally does not know the *content* of that condition. The man in search of the law in the short story under consideration; the man who is being punished but does not know why he is being punished in "*In the Penal Colony*"; the man who is trying to get into *The Castle* but does not know how; the man in *The Trial* who is served with papers to appear at a trial without being told of the accusation against him—in most cases, Kafka's fiction tells of a protagonist who is highly compelled but unaware exactly what his compulsion *is*.[4] Giorgio Agamben has accurately called this Kafkaesque predicament "being in force without significance."[5] There is a lot of force in Kafka's fiction. His protagonists are highly motivated. What the significance of their motivation is, though, is always difficult to discern.

It is striking to me how easy it is to discern this Kafkaesque quality in so many cases where authority is being enacted. Especially when *educational* authority is being enacted, such authority often borders on the Kafkaesque. I do not consider it a stretch to think about the many instances when educational authority impinges on students and teachers as instances that have "force without significance." From the student perspective, one need only think of the processes by which one obtains degrees, diplomas, and grades. As many a student can tell you, one works for a degree, perhaps for years and years. When the degree is finally obtained, there often lingers a certain dissatisfaction that the precise thing that one coveted for so long is really not much more than a shiny piece of paper with fancy print. One tends to wonder, in the end, if there was really any content to the very goal of all that travail. To be sure, on the way toward that goal, a student often projects into the degree, the diploma, or the certificate a magical sort of content. But in the end, haven't most students felt a sort of Kafkaesque realization that there was plenty of force to the degree, but not so much significance? This parallel between Kafkaesqueness and student experience seems to break down only insofar as Kafka's protagonists feel this lack of significance *even on the way toward* their goals. While in education, students usually sense that authority is hollow only once they have experienced the full dose of what authority has to offer, Kafka's characters are persecuted with such hollowness from the very beginning.

From the teacher's perspective, one might think of the authority enacted when grades are given. Haven't many teachers felt the intense irony of the grading procedure? To be sure, grading is one of the central processes by which teaching authority is enacted. But is there not a distinct lack of *content* to grading? While grades are, at least as far as institutional rhetoric is concerned, supposed to reflect the achievement of students, it is really very difficult to say that grades actually do such a thing. As most teachers would, I think, acknowledge, one never actually knows how much a student has, or has not, learned. A teacher can hardly hope to know some of the more intangible aspects of student learning, such as whether the student puts her learning to use some time in the future, or whether the student uses that learning to shape her future life in empowering ways.

Grades are also said to have significance insofar as they motivate students. But the final grade at the end of an academic semester, however full of force it is, is particularly lacking in such motivational significance. At such an endpoint, the grade can no longer serve its ostensible purpose as motivator because there is nothing to be motivated *for* when the course is already completed! And even when interim grades are given out, say, as the academic semester progresses, isn't there often a certain Kafkaesque sense in which the grades have a lot of force but very little content? Grades really do not *mean* much of anything. Many experienced teachers will say, if not in these precise terms, that they have felt a sort of Kafkaesque pang when they allot grades. As one long-time primary school teacher recently told me, "When it comes giving grades, I often feel like a charlatan."

Or, one can think about the forceful, yet content-less, quality that typifies the teaching of the famous educator Socrates. When, in the *Meno*, Socrates acts as a "torpedo fish," when he refuses to give content to his interlocutors but instead answers their questions with more questions of his own, he enacts the sort of educational authority that leaves them, much like the man in Kafka's story, without anywhere to go.[6] Or when Socrates says that he is the wisest of the Athenians because he knows not how *much* he knows, but rather how *little* he knows, he certainly enacts a very powerful—yet content-less—show of authority.[7]

And again, when in the *Meno* he uses his skill at questioning to evoke from the slave boy geometrical knowledge without teaching him anything *new*, there is a sense in which the authority of Socrates comes not from any meaning, but from some sort of pure force.

It *might* even be said that the Greek doctrine of *anamnesis*, far from being an obtuse and unbelievable myth of the existence of some collective memory, is more properly conceived as that enigmatic quality of educational authority that Kafka illustrates so well.[8] What I mean by this is that perhaps the Greeks noticed exactly what Kafka noticed about authority. Perhaps they noticed the many instances when authority seems to function even in the absence of propositional meaning. Upon noticing such a magical occurrence, it is not at all unreasonable, at least in a society where myths are common, to explain away such a thing with recourse to mythology. If meaning seems to come from nowhere, then the myth of collective memory is a fine way to explain just where "nowhere" is located. And another point is to be made about Socratic themes. Take the elenchus, or, "Socratic Method." The force of the enlenchus, with its refusal to give answers, with its refusal to give meaning—this force can well be described in the same way that Agamben describes Kafka's world. The enlenchus is full of "force without significance."

AUTHORITY AND THE LITERARY RELATION

So in Kafka's fiction, we can see the beginnings of an analysis of *how* the authority relation works. Following the examples of authority that fill the works of Kafka, I would say that educational authority most often works on the basis of a certain "force without significance." In order to further illustrate the force without significance of educational authority, it is helpful to look at Jacques Derrida's analysis of Kafka. Following Derrida, we can understand the force without significance of educational authority as the same sort of authority enacted through the reader's encounter with literature. The workings of authority are indebted to the sort of *relation* that occurs when one encounters literature. So in the case of "Before the Law," the man from the country is not only unsuccessful at understanding and gaining access to "the Law," where the law is an example of authority. In addition, the man from the country also typifies the reader of literature who does not understand, and thus cannot gain access to, a piece of literature. "The man from the country," writes Derrida, "had difficulty in grasping that an entrance was singular or unique when it should have been universal, as in truth it was. He had difficulty with literature."[9]

Derrida thus draws the helpful analogy between authority in general, and the authority of literature. He draws an analogy that helps to elucidate the precise distinction that I am, in this work, trying to make between authority that gets enacted relationally and other, more static, substance-oriented understandings of authority. Why did the man from the country have difficulty with the authority of literature? He had difficulty with it because he understood authority as a substance rather than as a relation. He thought it was some *thing* that lay in wait behind a closed door. Relating to authority, like relating to literature, can never be a matter of getting at some thing that a piece of literature "possesses."

WRONG APPROACHES TO LITERATURE

To repeat, I am trying to describe the authority relation as a literary one. There are, of course, good ways and bad ways to approach literature. Let me describe the bad ways because they will, later, help to shed some light on educational authority. There are three common, but mistaken, ways that people approach literature. First of all, there is the tendency to judge the authority of a literary work by its content. Oftentimes it is said that a great literary work is great because of the story it tells, because it is said to embody some universal human theme, because it has content that is authoritative. Yet, as any good reader of literature will tell us, such a content-bound judgment is bound to fail. Take, for example, two stories that are about the exact same thing, one that is judged "literary" and another that is not. It may very well be the case that the same "facts" that are included in a great piece of literature are also included in another, derivative piece of writing that is not considered literary. Content alone is never a guarantee that a piece of writing will be admitted into a literary canon.

Secondly, consider the attempt to judge the literary worth of a work by making an assessment based on the *form* of a piece. While it is often said that a literary work is distinguished by the *way* it is written, such a basis for judgment is also bound to fail. It may very well be the case that two works are written with the same flair, with the same voice. Still, their status as "literature" may be quite different. The authority of a piece of literature does not reside in its style alone. Style and form are easy to duplicate. As many a copycat author is aware, two works may be written in the same style, but even so, one of those two works, the one written by the copycat, may never end up being deemed literary. When it comes to discerning literary authority, the very thing that seems so central to a great piece of fiction—its style and its form— is not enough to provide an "entrance" for the work. Form, like content, is not a sufficient condition for the enactment of literary authority.

Remarking on the content and form of literary authority, Derrida reminds us that, in reality, the authority of literature lies elsewhere:

"What differs from one work to the other," notes Derrida, "is not its *content*, nor is it the *form* (the signifying expression, the phenomenon of language or rhetoric). It is the movements of framing and referentiality."[10] While content and form are both important, these elements alone, or even together, do not constitute the literary authority of a work. Why? Because "the movements of framing and referentiality" that indeed convince us that a work is authoritative cannot be so easily pinned down to one element or the other. Authority is not a "thing" to be found behind this "door" of content or that "door" of form. Rather, it is in the relation of "framing and referentiality" that the authority of literature resides. The authority of literature is always established in relation, in the relation that is established between readers and the literary works they read. It may be the case that content and form come into play as one deems a work to be great, but authority gets enacted more through the deeming than through the content or the form per se.

Third, there are often attempts made to assess literary authority by looking to authorship. As is the case with great content and great form, it is often assumed that a great author makes a work great. Hence, it might be said that William Faulkner's novels are among the great works of literature primarily because of Faulkner's status as a formidable novelist. This sort of assessment falls flat too, though. It may be the source of great consolation to the copycat author to sigh and say, "Well, I can write just as well as William Faulkner but I just lack the notoriety. I lack his great name." But while this sort of writerly resentment might massage the ego of a copycat, the truth of the matter is that Faulkner himself has written lesser works that have never been authorized with the status of "masterpiece." Many an author has written that "one great novel" only to fall into obscurity because his or her other works were never granted such "great" status. Who an author is is no guarantee of authority. Once again, authority does not reside "behind some door," at least not in the form of the author's identity.

So literary authority has "framing and referentiality" at its core, rather than the authoritative "things" of content, form, or authorship. When a person encounters literary authority, it is *unlikely* that one can discern the nature of that authority by scrutinizing *what it is* (its content) or *how it is presented* (its form) or *who is behind it*. As Derrida notes, "Thus one never acceded directly to the law or to persons, one is never *immediately* before any of these authorities; as for the detour, it may be infinite."[11] One never has *direct* access to literary authority. Faced with literary authority, one is primarily faced with the ways that such authority is instantiated in the people who enact, interpret, embody, and employ that authority. "One cannot reach the law, and in order to have a *rapport* of respect with it, *one must not* have a rapport with the law, *one must interrupt the relation*. One must *enter into relation* only with the law's representatives, its examples, its guardians."[12] In literature, as in education, authority is a relation of force without significance.

WRONG APPROACHES TO EDUCATION

But how does this Derridean understanding of literary authority inform, in a practical way, the matter of educational authority? Educational authority, I propose, is at present wrongly construed. At present, we tend to assess educational authority in the same mistaken ways that *bad* readers construe literary authority. We, too, try to look behind the "doors" of content, form, and authorship.

First, there is a common tendency to focus on content when it comes to questions of authority. As I have outlined earlier in this study, many serious analyses of educational authority focus mainly on the role of content, on the role of the texts that are taught by teachers. Many such analyses deem educational authority to be "great" when the texts that are taught are "great." Such an orientation toward "great" curriculum guides the progressive, traditional, and critical perspectives alike. Following the progressive program of education, authority is doing the right thing when teachers get out of the way and let great texts speak for themselves. Following the traditional program, authority is valid when it is used to shore up the knowledge embodied in great texts. Following the critical program, authority is valid when great texts are understood in ways that debunk hegemonic ideology. Yet, what these perspectives on authoritative content overlook is that content per se cannot possibly be the source of educational authority. If content were a sufficient source of educational authority, then education as we know it would not even be necessary. What I mean by this is that one can find "great" texts almost anywhere: in libraries, in bookstores, online, on the shelves of studies, living rooms, and bedrooms. Anyone can read a great text anywhere. The mere fact that one has read a great text hardly signifies that educational authority has been enacted.

There is also a common tendency to judge educational authority by virtue of its form. That is to say, there is a tendency to judge authority by looking to the quality of instruction. This sort of judgment has its pitfalls as well. It is by no means true that a teacher who has carried out his or her lesson in the best manner has necessarily contributed at all to the education of even one student! As many a teacher will testify, all of the best techniques are bound to fall on deaf ears at one point or another. Quite simply, there is no one teaching style, and there is not even any specific combination of teaching styles, which will guarantee that one's students become well educated. In spite of all the technicist, rationalist, optimistic educational research into the ways that education can be delivered more effectively by teachers, there is simply no guarantee that "good" instruction will suffice. Authority can never be judged by quality of instruction because quality of instruction is itself a dubious notion. As in the case of the copycat author who tries to copy the work of a master writer, there is no certainty that copying the "best practices" of other teachers will lead to an educative experience on the part of the student.

Too, there is a mistaken tendency to judge educational authority by its author, by who does the teaching. Let me bring in my own observations here, as a teacher of nineteen years. Over the years as I have listened to many students talk about their teachers, the one thing that always rings true is that the authority of any particular teacher always differs according that teacher's particular relation to particular students. It is not uncommon for a teacher with certain highly idiosyncratic pedagogical techniques to win a highly prestigious award for university teaching. Often, this very teacher is detested by as many students as she is loved. Her idiosyncrasies are harmful as well as helpful. Educational authority cannot be attributed to authorship, to the teacher, in any consistent way at all. Quite simply, one student's super-teacher is often another's worst teacher. This is just as sure as the fact that the author of one great novel is likely to write a flop now and again.

Like the authority of literature, education authority tends to be judged by content, form, and authorship—by curriculum, technique, and teacher identity. Yet when we so judge educational authority, we make the same mistake that an ill-informed reader of literature makes. We make the mistake of looking for authority "behind some door" as if it is a substance or a thing just waiting to be revealed. When we so judge educational authority, we ignore the fact that authority must be construed as a relation. It must, as Derrida says, be construed as a matter of "framing and referentiality." If we treat educational authority as a relation akin to the literary relation, then we must look past the individual qualities that texts, pedagogies, and teachers are said to "possess." We must look at the "force" of such a relation rather than its "significance." We must look at its movements rather than at its steadfast qualities. We must examine *how it reads* rather than *what it is*.

THEN WE ARE ALL FROM THE COUNTRY

So let us return to Kafka's story. It seems that we can now describe the countryman as a sort of student. The man stands before the law in much the same way a student stands before educational authority. In this new version of Kafka's tale, we might say that there is a student who is barred entrance to authority. Why is he barred entrance? It is because he mistakenly thinks that the primary attribute of educational authority is that it is generally available. He thinks that authority is somewhere within, that it is written inside on a tablet, like some moral code.[13] He believes that if only he is patient enough, then he will be let in and will be able to discern authority's true content. But, this student of Kafka's can never gain entry into the house of educational authority. He remains frustrated. He never learns that in reality authority has no specific content. In truth, it has no identifiable form. This student's misunderstanding of the nature of authority leads to his continued desire to get through an open door. This student has a problem with educational authority in the same way that many people "have a problem with literature." He believes that it is his role to figure out exactly "what" authority is.

It is a mistake on the part of the student to think that facing authority entails facing a canon of knowledge that is already there. It is a mistake to think that a particular body of knowledge is waiting to be understood in a particular way. When faced with authority, one should not ask to gain such straightforward entrance. One will never gain such an entrance. Instead, one should understand that authority has no steadfast life. It has no "truth" that is set in stone behind a door. Authority is always a movement that can never be pinned down. It is a movement between content, form, and teacher. Because authority is a movement, the student must understand that he will never be able to gain *direct* entrance. But if our student can never gain direct entrance, then what *can* he do? Or to put this question in more broad terms: How might students and teachers negotiate the relation of authority given that it has such a literary life?

Rather than trying to gain direct entrance, a student might do much better to engage in the very staging of authority, to engage in its referentiality, to engage in the effects it has on him or herself. A student might understand that confronting education is much like gaining access to a great novel. To access the authority of a novel, one does not dwell strictly on its content, nor does one dwell strictly on its form, nor does one dwell strictly on what so-and-so (say, a teacher) says about the novel. Let us say, for example, that this student is a reader of James Joyce. To read and interpret Joyce's *Ulysses*, it is absolutely insufficient to understand its content. Its content is, after all, only one life in the day of a fairly unremarkable man, Leopold Bloom. To read and interpret *Ulysses*, it is also completely insufficient to know that, in its form, *Ulysses* is a metaphor for Homer's epic poem. To read and interpret *Ulysses*, it is furthermore insufficient to learn precisely who James Joyce, the writer, was. Likewise, it is insufficient to learn precisely what Dr. X, the professor, has to say about the novel. To read and interpret *Ulysses*, one must engage in a relation with all of the factors that allow one to be moved by the reading. One must enjoy the story. One must make one's own judgments about its worth. One must arrive at an interpretion of the novel in a way that is ultimately unlikely to be the same interpretation that one finds somewhere in some certain place, behind some door.

This student would do well to proceed without the illusion that *Ulysses*, just because it has been assigned for a course, has some authority that is thing-ified or concrete. This student would do well to take an example from many a devoted novel reader. It is not a coincidence that many readers of novels do so late at night in the comfort of their bedrooms, and indeed that they do not discuss the contents of the novel with anyone else. The successful interpreter of a novel ultimately meets the authority of the novel through his or her own personal acts of "staging and referentiality." Reading a novel successfully, one will enter a personal relation with the mechanisms of literary authority. One will enter into a relation with the authority that canonizes novels and satisfies readers. One will enter a personal relation with the "doorkeepers" of literary insight rather than coming to know precisely "what" or "who" they are.

Any student who encounters classroom curriculum should proceed in this same literary light. Faced with a way to "enter" curriculum, the student might best be aware that it will not be solely a matter of knowing the content of what is being taught. Nor will it be strictly a matter of knowing the *form* of curriculum, of being taught correctly. Nor will it be strictly a matter of having direct access to the author, of having direct access to the teacher. In fact one does not "enter" curriculum in such a straightforward way. Rather, one must enter an interpretive relation wherein the person who learns acts as her own guide, as her own literary interpreter, doing her own "staging" and her own establishing of "referentiality."

This is not to say that the learner should not look to outside sources in order to interpret curriculum. Indeed, it may be precisely by means of outside sources that a student finds insight that will bear on her own interpretations. One may go to a teacher. One may go to a text of reference. One may go to a dictionary. One may go to a friend, to an instructional text, to a text of criticism, etc. But while it may be in one of these sources where one finds the means to stage an interpretation, it will never be in these sources where one reaches some authoritative source. Authority in education is a relation that gets enacted in the interpretive act itself, in the act of learning. It is not a thing that lies hidden waiting to be found. A student will never "reach" educational authority, but he or she does have the chance, like the reader of a novel, to stage an event of curriculum that becomes meaningful and enriching. Like the novel reader who is transformed because of her own personal interpretation of a work, the student's own interpretation of curriculum is the only way that she can partake in the relation of authority. This is not to say she will "enter the house" of authority. She will, though, achieve a *relation* with one or more of its doorkeepers.

THE TEACHER AND THE LITERARY RELATION

But if the student never has direct access to authority, does that mean that the teacher *does* have direct access? Not at all. A literary understanding throws into question many current assumptions about the educational authority of the teacher. For example, educational accounts of authority often assume that a teacher who has more authority is one who does a lot more direct instruction of content. It is often said that dialogic pedagogies or progressive pedagogies are able to eschew authority because they do not force-feed students with content. Informed by our literary understanding of authority, this is simply wrongheaded. Authority can never reside in the content itself, nor in that content's delivery. This very popular, scholarly-accepted perspective makes the same mistake as Kafka's countryman made. It assumes that authority lies behind the door. It assumes that authority is sequestered knowledge. Scholarly arguments about whether or not to use such "authority" will never get anywhere because they misconstrue the way that authority is necessarily an interpretive relation. Such descriptions of teacher authority are as ill-conceived as are the notions of the student who assumes she can access that venerable, carved-in-stone version of authority.

The authority of the teacher does not depend upon the extent of the teacher's knowledge, nor does it depend upon the approach the teacher takes to his or her subject, nor does it depend upon who the teacher is. Haven't many teachers had the same experience that the countryman has had? Is it not a common feeling to be barred entrance to teaching authority? Are there not many times when one just can't get through to one's students? I, for one, have felt like the countryman. With regard to content: How often do we wrongly assume that if the content is clear, then the rest of teaching and learning will take care of itself? After a feeling of being barred entrance, many teachers make the following content-based mistake: they just try all the harder to make the content clear to their students. With regard to teaching methods: How often do we wrongly assume that some innovative approach to teaching will make learning possible where none was possible before? With regard to teacher identity: How often do we wrongly assume that a teacher lacks authority because he is too young, because he is has not established a good enough reputation, because he is not as likeable as another teacher of the same course? Yet how many teachers never become successful when in fact their reputation and experience should have gained them "entrance" long ago? When teaching the novels of Toni Morrison, for example, one can know all there is to know about Morrison. One can polish up one's teaching style to be as shiny as can be. One can have years and years of experience. These matters of content, form, and identity do not guarantee that a student's interpretation of Morrison will be profound. Matters of content, form, and identity will not guarantee a teacher access to authority because authority is not a particular thing waiting to be accessed.

Authority only gets enacted through a meaningful interpretation on the student's part. It is the student who must actually practice the "staging and referentiality" of this interpretation. The best that the teacher can do is to act as an aid to the reader. Of course, it may happen that it is precisely the content knowledge or the teaching style of the teacher that the student uses to make her interpretation meaningful. Or it may not happen that way. If, at least, a teacher knows that content, style, and identity are not sufficient, then he or she will not make the same mistake as Kafka's countryman. He or she will not continue to expect that the aim of the teacher is to "let in" the student. As teachers, we should not aim to "give over" authority, nor should we aim to "keep" our authority. Authority is not a substance that one "has." The best we can do is to avoid making the same mistake as the man from the country. We can avoid trying to "get through" to our students. And, we can help students to avoid making the same mistake by pointing out that they will never "get through" to us. They will never "get through" to some illusory authority that the teacher is supposed to "have."

Does all this mean that we can no longer talk about the content of teaching? Can we no longer talk about pedagogy? Can we no longer talk about the charisma of the teacher? This is not my point at all. Indeed, texts are central (as I have argued in the previous chapter), pedagogy is absolutely necessary, and teacher charisma a boon. Of the three, I would say that texts are the most important. But . . . this choice has nothing to do with the authority that might wrongly considered to be inherent in any one of the three. Rather, the text is preferable to the other two because it is more likely to lend itself to *interpretation*. The texts that teachers teach are preferable because they are already situated within a set of discursive practices that encourage reading and interpretation, *not* because of some mistaken stereotype of a pure, nonauthoritative experience of knowledge acquisition on the part of the student. Given the deferred, interpretive life of a student's interaction with texts, the act of reading is more likely to enable one to participate in the literary life of educational authority. Teachers should favor texts, but this is not because texts are some "source" of authority. Texts are not behind the door. They remain in front of it. Teachers, like students, should settle for the foyer. To be let in need not be the aim.

To recap, I have so far offered a description of authority that asks us to stop thinking of authority as a matter of substance, style, and identity, and asks us to start thinking of it as a matter of interpretation and reading. There is no stable, authoritative meaning behind the door over which the doorkeeper stands guard. There is actually no way to enter the room guarded by the doorkeeper. The entranceway itself is the venue where one learns, where one becomes educated. The entranceway is also where one teaches. One can't "get in." One can at best, one can only, enter a relation with the doorkeeper. When the doorkeeper (or the teacher) says to the man (or to the student), "This door was intended only for you," it makes sense to settle for the door.

BUT WHY DO WE ASSUME THAT SOME THING IS BEHIND THE DOOR?

All of this said, why is it such a common presumption that authority is located somewhere in particular? Why are there so many countrymen among us who assume that authority is a "thing" that is waiting somewhere behind a door? Why do people ignore the interpretive life of the authority relation? To get at an answer to this question, I want to look to language itself. For it seems to me that common presumptions about authority are actually based on even more fundamental presumptions about what it means to speak and to listen. That is to say, because authority is most often *communicated*, there are some very deep presumptions about communication itself that tend to derail how we understand authority. Communication itself is much more of an interpretive event than is commonly realized. Therefore, when authority is construed as a substance rather than an interpretive relation, this misunderstanding is itself guided by a misunderstanding of language where language is said to be the transfer of a *substance* between autonomous human actors, that substance being *meaning*.

To this end, I take a bit of a detour through language theory in the pages that follow. Once we understand that communication is *not* solely about the transfer of meaning, but is rather a matter of authoritative staging and interpretation, then we can see that the relation of authority is indeed literary from the ground up, from the very basic acts of listening and speaking all the way up to the more refined enactments of educational authority that take place between student and teacher.

THE SENDER-RECEIVER MODEL

One of the most common ways to understand human communication is according to the "sender-receiver" model. Following such a model, it is assumed that language is a tool, a "thing," that is used by human actors to communicate with one another. As such, when human beings have ideas, they use the tool of language to send their ideas to one another. John Stewart has argued that this tool-like understanding of language has been one of the primary philosophical commitments to which philosophers of language have adhered. He describes this "tool commitment" as follows:

> Historically, of course, the primary use of the language tool has been viewed as the communication of thoughts or ideas. Among others, Locke underscored the importance of the communicative function of language, and the eighteenth-century theorist John Horne Tooke would not even grant "language" status to the solitary mental naming that some of his predecessors had analyzed. Horne Tooke argued that the fact that the purpose of language is "to communicate our thoughts" should "be kept singly in contemplation . . ."[14]

George Lakoff and Mark Taylor, commenting on how many people talk of language, describe the use of the "conduit metaphor."[15] According to this metaphorical description of language, "The speaker puts ideas (objects) into words (containers) and sends them (along a conduit) to a hearer who takes the idea/object out of the word/containers." It is the sending and the receiving part of this metaphor that I would like to highlight. It is not only in high philosophy, but it is in our everyday speech, too, where the sender-receiver model is assumed. As Taylor notes, the following sorts of conduit metaphors are used all the time: "It's hard to *get* that idea *across to* him"; "Your reasons *came through* to us"; and, "I *gave* you that idea."[16] These are just a few examples of many other common ways of talking that echo the sender-receiver conception of language.

So according to the sender-receiver model, human beings first have something in mind to communicate. They put their thoughts into language, into words, and then those words are sent to other human beings. The process of communication, then, is often construed as if we communicate via something like a pneumatic tube. First a person thinks a thought. Then that person puts that thought into words. The persons then sends those words to another person via pneumatic tube. The person at the other end of the communication receives those words. He or she deciphers those words, and thus understands what was on the sender's mind. According to this sender-receiver model, it is assumed that language communicates a world of ideas that can easily be transmitted from one person to another.

The sender-receiver model of communication is well ensconced in a modernist, Enlightenment conception of human beings as autonomous actors. Following this conception, a person is an atomistic entity who has ideas, thoughts, intentions, and ambitions. A person can exist just fine on his or her own. In fact, the Enlightenment conception of the self insists that people *should* exist on their own. As Stewart notes of the tool orientation toward language, "[T]he contemporary emphasis on language as an instrumental tool reflects the Cartesian cogito and the irreducible distinction between the subject and the objects that subjects allegedly encounter, construct, and manipulate."[17] And as I have pointed out with respect to Kant, the enlightened person is encouraged to think, act, and live autonomously. It is through the use of one's own reason, as opposed to living through a reliance on the guidance of others, that one rises from a state of immaturity to a state of maturity.

Of course, the Enlightenment conception of self does not object to people communicating with one another. People must communicate in order to live happy lives. Not even a stereotyped version of Kant's autonomous, "mature" person could be said to live without communicating with others. This is where the sender-receiver model of communication fits so well with Enlightenment notions of autonomy. According to the sender-receiver model, people need not be in reciprocal or mutually enhancing relations in order to communicate. Rather, people can stand at a fair distance from one another. The pneumatic tube acts as a buffer between people. One person has her thoughts and another person has her thoughts. They learn about each other's thoughts by means of the tool of language. Language enables one to learn what another person is thinking. After learning what the other is thinking, one can use one's own reason, one's enlightened "mature" reason, to decide which path to take.

The sender-receiver model is a modernist, Enlightenment model. Alphonso Lingis has underscored this fact by describing the sender-receiver model of communication as the sort that takes place in modern, "rational communities."[18] For Lingis, there are two main types of communities: rational communities and communities of difference. It is in the former type of community that communication is thought of according to the sender-receiver model. In what Lingis calls rational communities, people gather together on the assumption that they have something in common to say to each other. People gather together because they believe that they all share a common enough language to understand the various ideas, the various viewpoints, that various members of the rational community have. Lingis notes the following about the rational community of communication:

> Each one speaks as a representative of the common discourse. His own insights and utterances become part of the anonymous discourse of universal reason.
>
> This discursive practice then invokes a human community in principle unlimited. A community in which each one, in facing the other, faces an imperative that he formulate all his encounters and insights in universal terms, in forms that could be the information belonging to everyone.[19]

In the rational community, which is the sort of community that the modern, liberal state is based on, people use the public sphere to "send messages" to one another in a common language. Thus, the very idea of the modern, rational community is based on the assumption that language is the public tool that will be used to send ideas that can be understood by all as long as those ideas are communicated well enough. When I send a message about an idea that I have in mind, that message will, in a rational community, be understandable to many, many people. Many people will be able to share in the common language that conveys my meaning.

Three important observations are to be made about the authority relation and the sender-receiver model of communication. The first is this: common understandings of authority are based on this same simplistic sender-receiver model of communication. That is to say, authority is usually treated as if it is the bearer of a message. When people talk about authority, and when they theorize about it, they refer to a person who "has" authority. It is assumed that such a person communicates her ideas to someone who does not "have" such authority. It is further assumed that if the person communicates her ideas well enough to the other, then that other can "get" authority if she has understood clearly. My point here is that the sender-receiver metaphor about how language communicates ideas is the same metaphor that guides common presumptions about how authority gets "passed" from one person to another. Just as people assume that some specific idea gets transferred through each utterance, so, too, people assume that some specific type of authority can be transferred through an utterance.

The second observation follows from the concept of the rational community to which Lingis introduces us. It is this: when a person is said to "have" authority, then it is assumed that his or her authority can be understood by many people. It is assumed that such authority is able to be understood by the members of a rational community who share a common language. Just as in the case of person's ideas that are "sent" by language to all who share that common language, so too is it assumed that authority exists within a "rational community" whose interlocutors are able to understand one another. Authority, like an idea that one sends to another in a rational community of one common language, is assumed to make sense to a lot of people.

I want to illustrate this by way of an example from my own teaching. Yet, I am sure that my own experience is hardly unique. As a university professor, I sometimes expound in class upon some of my own ideas. Oftentimes students ask me questions about those ideas. Tellingly, even when I state that those are *my own* ideas, students go on to ask where they can do further reading about those ideas. I will say it again: in spite of my claim that these are my own unique ideas, students very often insist that they want other sources to go to in order to learn more about those ideas! Now, by giving this example, I am not trying to belittle my students in any way. Indeed, a student who wants to do further study about some educational concept that I raise is the very sort of student I, for one, want to be teaching. However, this student who insists that my own ideas must have origins elsewhere does so because she assumes that there must be some rational community from which my ideas emanate. She assumes that there must be some common language that she has not been exposed to yet. Indeed, many students assume that there must be some common rational community of scholars who authorize the speaking teacher.

As will have been guessed by now, I am no fan of the sender-receiver model of rational communication. Here is a third observation: this model contradicts itself. The contradiction is this: even when authority is ostensibly denounced, the specter of authority always returns in the form of an assumed rational community. Even when the Enlightenment model of communication eschews authority, it advocates a common language that is, itself, a forceful form of authority. So the Kantian imperative to "have the courage to think on your own" depends upon a rational community that does not let one think on one's own! Let me say this a different way. Think about the students of mine who want to find out where I "really" get my ideas. Because they assume that there is a rational community behind my speaking, my speaking can never become "mature." Like good Kantians, they know that one can never speak on one's own. Yet also like good Kantians, they want me to be an authority in my own right. The Enlightenment sender-receiver model assumes that we all rely on the authority of the rational community at the same time that it eschews reliance on authority.

So back to the question, "But why do we think some *thing* is behind the door?" In order to explain this resilient belief, I have tried

to explicate some of the erroneous communicative assumptions surrounding authority. People tend to think that there is some *thing* behind
the door in the same way that people tend to think that there is some
person's idea behind each word that is spoken. People tend to think that
authority is a substance because they cling to the modernist belief that
if authority is being communicated then there must be some specific
"thing" that is being sent to someone else.

People tend to think that there is some thing behind the door
because they tend to think that communication arises from an established rational community. Going back to the example of my own students who, when I am talking about my own ideas, make the assumption
that there must be some rational community somewhere from which I
am speaking, it seems that people both want to get away from authority
and at the same time want to insist that there is, after all, some "rational" authority that one cannot get away from. No matter how much
one wishes to be mature, one still assumes that the key to maturity is
just behind somebody else's door. This happens because people assume
that communication is rational and that communication is mainly about
ideas that lie in wait to be understood.

Two questions follow from this discussion, and I will address these
questions by way of concluding this chapter on the literary life of authority. The first is: Is there an alternative model of communication? Is
there one that is different from the sender-receiver model, one that
better describes how relational authority works? The second is: If there
is such an alternative model, how, exactly, does it help us to understanding the educational relation of authority?

AUTHORITY AND PERFORMATIVE COMMUNICATION

In contrast to the sender-receiver model of communication, we should
rather think of authority according to a model of performative communication. Such a model can be distinguished from a sender-receiver model
in a number of ways, some of which I will outline here. To begin with,
a performative model construes that *the saying itself* is just as important
as *what is said*. Take for example the utterance of a teacher. When a
teacher speaks, there is certainly something in particular that is being
said by her. Yet at the same time, it is the speaking itself that establishes
a relation between herself and her class of students. Following the sender-
receiver model, we might have assumed that *what is said* by the teacher
is the most important thing, that the most important thing is the thought
that is communicated to the class. In contrast, a performative account
of communication helps us to understand that the speaking itself is
important. The performative model helps us to remember that when a

teacher addresses her class, she establishes a role by her very speaking. She may be taking roll. She may be giving a lesson no one understands. She may have taught some mathematics skill without knowing exactly how she got her point across. Whatever the case, the relation between her and her students will most often be established by *the fact that she has said something* rather than *what she has said*.

The performative model of communication differs in another major way from the sender-receiver model. In the sender-receiver model, it is assumed that a clear and consistent understanding of the speaker's intent is the most important aspect of communication. On the performative model, though, it is assumed that differences in understanding are just as important as consistencies in understanding. So when someone says something to me, one way of looking at what has been said is that it is my job to understand (and to understand correctly) what has been said to me. But another way of looking at communication is to realize that my interpretation of what has been said may very well *never* be quite the same as what the speaker intended to mean.

Following a performative model of communication, it is not a *problem* that I have not understood exactly what the speaker had in mind. Such a misunderstanding is part and parcel of what it means to communicate. Indeed, as Hans-Georg Gadamer has intimated, every understanding is also, in part, a misunderstanding.[20] According to the performative model, it cannot be the role of language to transport via pneumatic tube, safely and securely, the intended meaning of one speaker to the attentive ears of her listener. Why? Because language operates as much on misunderstanding as it does on understanding. It may be that a listener *mis*understands a speaker as much as she understands him. A sender-receiver conception of communication might hold at this point that the two have not communicated. From the performative perspective, this sort of phenomenon *is still communication*. It is perhaps the most common version of communication.

Furthermore, the performative perspective acknowledges that there are many circumstances when communication takes place not because of the knowledge that someone has in mind but because of the unique, perlocutionary circumstances that surround that communication.[21] In other words, sometimes communication happens because of the circumstances of the speaker and listener rather than because of any specific knowledge that is conveyed from one to the other. The quintessential example of this, offered by J. L. Austin, is when a minister pronounces a couple "husband and wife." When a minister does so, the *effect* of the pronouncement does not depend upon the knowledge or understanding of the speaker and his or her listeners. Rather, the *effect* depends upon staging and referentiality. It depends upon the circumstances surrounding what the minister has to say. It depends upon how the minister's words get interpreted.

It is not difficult to see how much the performative conception of communication bears on educational authority. If authority is relational, it is precisely because authority gets enacted in a performative, rather than a sender-receiver, way. Let me go back to the example of the teacher who takes roll, who teaches a lesson that is not clear to her students, or who has taught a math skill while not knowing exactly how she got her point across. When a teacher takes roll, it is truly not *what is said* that is important, at least not as far as authority is concerned. What is important when roll is taken is *that something is said*. As far as authority is concerned, there is little import whether the student whose name is called out is present or absent on that particular day. Of little import is whether or not the name called out is the name of a student who never planned to attend class. Of little import is whether or not the name that is called is a mistaken name, one generated by a computer glitch. Of little import is whether or not the teacher makes up a fictitious name to call and then calls that name in order to dupe the students in the class. As far as authority goes, the specific content of the roll call does not bear on the fact that the roll was called by a teacher and that students were listeners to that roll call. Authority gets enacted—with all its absences, presences, and potential mistakes— because roll was called, because a relation was established. It hardly matters that some name in particular, or even some "correct" name, was said during the roll call.

A performative understanding of authority thus helps us to understand the many instances when a teacher teaches a lesson that is not clear. If we were to cling to the sender-receiver model of authority, it might follow that authority has not succeeded, that it is somehow lessened, when a teacher is not able to communicate what she wants to communicate. This is simply not so: authority does not increase or decrease in direct proportion to what is learned "correctly" in the classroom. There are very often cases where much is learned that was not intended. In an English class, there might be an insightful reading of a piece of literature that is based on what the student *thought* the teacher said rather than what the teacher actually said. In a science class, there might be a mistaken, but nevertheless sensible, interpretation of the reasons behind an eclipse of the moon. In a math class, there might be an algorithm learned "incorrectly," an algorithm that solves the given math problem just as well. In any of these cases, as in many others where misunderstanding causes an understanding of its own, it can in no way be said that the enactment of authority has been lessened by such a misunderstanding. The relation of authority functions as much on misunderstanding as on understanding. As in instances of performative communication, it is the learning from another person, no matter what has been learned, for right or for wrong, that constitutes the relation of authority.

Take the example of a math teacher who, after trying to no avail to teach a certain mathematical technique to a particular student, decides to use other, affective means to inspire this student: "You are great at mathematics. Don't give up just because I'm not having one of my best teaching days!" In instances such as this, at least when they do turn out to be successful, it seems as though education happens through osmosis, or maybe by magic. However it happens, one is often hard-pressed to come up with a logical solution. In instances such as this, there is a striking similarity, if not an equivalence, between the educational relation of authority and the performative moment of authorization described by Austin. When the minister says, "I pronounce you married," and the teacher says, "You are great at mathematics," the same performative event results, or at least it can result if the circumstances are "felicitous."[22] Just as two partners "become" married by virtue of this pronouncement, it is altogether possible that a student will "become" great by virtue of what the teacher has said to him or her. Or at least (in a less momentous sense), it may be the case that the student will become "great" enough to learn the mathematics in spite of the teacher's inadequate methods. In such cases, it is the performative relation that typifies the workings of authority, even when there may be no sender-receiver explanation for the learning that took place.

Eric Santner, for example, has noted the following about performativity, especially in a literary context:

> [A] work is endowed with a life beyond the order of knowledge, beyond a merely additive history of tastes and style. Such "redemptive" reading can, to borrow the language of speech-act theory, never be reduced to a purely constative act of noting the positive features of the work but depends instead on a dimension of performativity.[23]

In this passage, Santner is describing the way that works of literature can bring human beings to new levels of awareness. As Santner notes, literature brings such new levels of awareness in a performative way. Literary works are "endowed with a life beyond the order of knowledge," beyond what one can say about content and style. I would add to Santner's comments that education works in the same performative way. Educational authority calls to us in ways that bring new levels of awareness. Teachers and students are also "endowed with a life beyond the order of knowledge."

Santner goes on to describe how each performative reading of a work is different from its previous reading:

> What makes a work of art inexhaustible, subject to multiple interpretations, is not simply an excess of content or information that, because of the limits of every human consciousness, requires multiple readings to "bring it out"; rather, this much noted inexhaustibility depends on the fact that every reading is, on a certain level, a kind of *creation ex nihilo*. The details supporting a strong reading of a work only become visible retroactively, in light of the performative gesture that intervenes into its history of reception. In a certain sense, these details were not there before . . .[24]

Let me put Santner's thoughts in terms of educational authority. In education, what makes the experience of learning inexhaustible is not the vast content that the teacher might bring into the classroom day after day. It is not the ability of the teacher to encourage students to think in many different ways about that vast content. The inexhaustibility of authority rests rather in the way in which something can be created from scratch when teacher and student meet. When teacher and student meet in order to study something, a performative gesture "intervenes." In a sense, certain details of the curriculum may not have been there before this intervention. Or, to go back to a phrase that I have used earlier, through the performative intervention of authority, teacher and student "become the missing pages" of the text that is taught.

Indeed, it is necessary to look beyond the sender-receiver model of communication. Authority is a relation that acts performatively. Therefore, authority gets enacted through interpretation rather than through clear communication. It is not that someone "has" authority and then communicates her ideas clearly by virtue of that authority. Instead, authority gets enacted through communication itself. It gets enacted through the communicative relation. Authority depends more on *the being said* than it depends on *what is said*. This becomes obvious when we notice that authority gets enacted through misunderstanding as often as it gets enacted through understanding.

Looking beyond the sender-receiver model of communication brings us full circle, back to the countryman in front of Kafka's door. The countryman assumes that there is some authority figure behind the door. He assumes that there is a person who "has" authority. The man assumes that this person will communicate something to him. The countryman wants to be the receiver of a message that will be sent by this authority figure. The countryman does not understand that authority is a relation that acts performatively rather than through some sender-receiver model.

When a person takes part in the relation of educational authority, it is the relation itself that educates. It is the relation, rather than some predetermined content. One becomes educated through the interplay of content, style, and identity. One becomes educated through interpretation rather than through clarity. And the interpretation to which I am referring is particularly literary. Of course, to say that "the relation itself educates" is to force another matter into play. Namely, we must ask whether people must be *present* during this relation. Is it possible to have an authority relation when an authority figure is absent? This question will guide the chapter that follows.

CHAPTER 3

Relating to Authority Figures Who Are Not There

So far in this book I have dealt with relation in terms of authority figures who are *present*. However, when we think about the authority figures to whom we relate, don't we have relations with many who have left the picture? Are we not constantly relating to authority figures whom we remember? Whom we anticipate meeting in the future? Whom we know about but only rarely come into contact with? Indeed, might it be the case that we do *more* relating to those authority figures who are absent than to those who are present? In this chapter, I will investigate this particularly *lingering* aspect of the educational authority. I will argue that what lingers is actually central to educational authority. Absence has bearing on presence. And contrariwise, I maintain that presence has bearing on absence. Non-presence and presence are two symbiotic components of authority.

Let me draw on one example of absence from my own education: I was first introduced to the novelist Toni Morrison during my undergraduate education, in a course taught by Professor Denise Depuis. Under the thoughtful guidance of Professor Depuis, I came to cherish Morrison's writing, and especially her famous novel *Beloved*. Indeed, from the time of that course up until now, even when I am not in the presence of Professor Depuis, the warm image of her comes flooding back to mind each time I pick up a book written by Toni Morrison.

There are certainly variations on this sort of experience. Perhaps one learns to run, with grace and style, under the watchful eyes of a certain coach Hoffman. And then from time to time, when venturing to the park for just a short jog, the memory of coach Hoffman and his running tips hovers in the mind's eye, reminding one that a swifter run is always in store by letting the shoulders hang low, by keeping the fingers relaxed. Or maybe it's the memory of the person from whom one learned to play chess, or perhaps it is one's mathematics teacher, or one's philosophy of education instructor. If one has indeed gone through a truly educative experience in the presence of a teacher, isn't there often a parallel experience that is once removed from that teacher, a lingering memory of that teacher even though we are no longer in his or her presence?

THE PRESENTIST FALLACY

Unfortunately, current educational accounts of authority are hamstrung by a markedly *presentist* orientation.[1] A presentist orientation tends to address authority as if authority is always in the ideal state of being around. The presentist orientation focuses on instances when students are *face-to-face* with the authority of the teacher. Lost in this face-to-face focus is an account of the ways that authority reverberates *after* the classroom experience. There are a number of drawbacks to the presentist orientation, some of which I want to mention here. First, it ignores the fact that I have been trying to explain above, the fact that people are often affected by the authority relation when authority figures go away then come back, or when they go away permanently. Second, because the presentist orientation focuses on authority as if it is present, the nuances of difference between absent and present authority are lost.

    Most damagingly, the presentist orientation runs into the following dilemma: On the one hand, it is naïve to say that the authority relation stays around, *in the exact same form as if it were still present,* when the student and teacher are no longer in each other's company. On the other hand, it is equally naïve to say that authority needs little attention since the harm it causes, or the good it does, are only temporary. In the first case, we would be saying that every student is affected for a lifetime by each authority with whom he or she comes into contact. The first conclusion is certainly wrong: many students go through an entire course of twelve, sixteen, or more years of education being little, if at all, affected by those who are in positions of educational authority. The second conclusion is equally wrong: many people are affected in permanent ways by an authority figure who has gone away. A presentist orientation gets stuck between the Scylla of permanent presence and the Charybdis of permanent absence.

    But what happens when the two polar opposite presentist assumptions about authority (that face-to-face authority remains, as if present, indefinitely, or, conversely, that authority has force only when students

are face-to-face with teachers) are inadequate? Between these two extreme presentist assumptions, how might we consider the effects of authority that is present at some times and absent at others? How might we
describe authority that sometimes lingers and sometimes does not? How
might we describe a more complex interaction between the presence and
absence of authority? What happens when we leave the presentist orientation behind, and look at the life of the authority relation that comes
and goes, that has *various* effects in its comings and goings?

ABSENT AUTHORITY, PYCHIC PRESENCE

For anyone who knows a bit about psychoanalysis, it will be clear that
we are delving into matters of the psyche. Key concepts in psychoanalysis help to explain the force of authority figures who are not around.
Psychoanalytic concepts given to us by Freud, concepts such as transference, countertransference, the Oedipal struggle, melancholia—these
and many more psychoanalytic notions deal with the relations we have
with authority figures who have left the picture. Transference: when one
relates to a new authority figure in the same way one used to relate to
a similar figure in the past. Countertransference: when an authority
figure relates to a person not in authority the same way he or she has
done with another such person in the past. The Oedipal struggle: the
struggle that a child has with a parental authority figure, a struggle that
has repercussions throughout one's life even when the parent is not
around. Melancholia: when a deceased authority figure casts a bleak
shadow over the life of one who mourns.[2]

Indeed, I find that the best lens one can use to look into authority
figures who are no longer around is a psychoanalytic one. And so this
chapter will be indebted to a particular psychoanalytic viewpoint, the
viewpoint of Jessica Benjamin.[3] Benjamin's work offers an understanding of how educational authority might actually straddle the spaces of
presence *and* non-presence. As Benjamin reminds us, the experience of
an other may at first be a matter of being with that other. But ultimately, it is also a matter of *not* being with the other. Benjamin's work
helps to flesh out the relation between people who experience authority
in various ways, in absence as well as in presence.

Let us begin with presence and work our way toward absence.
According to Benjamin, the circuit of recognition is inaugurated when
the newborn looks up at the face of the caregiver in search of a warm,
confirming presence. In these first instances of life, the young person
learns the significance of the caretaker's presence. The caretaker's presence becomes a comforting one, one that will encourage both agency
and autonomy on the part of the child. When the child goes to play

with a toy, for example, she often looks for recognition from an authority figure. Notes Benjamin, "Now, when the infant reaches excitedly for a toy, he looks up to see if mother is sharing his excitement; he gets the meaning when she says, 'Wow!' "[4] In the caretaker's presence, the child derives encouragement and agency as the caretaker offers proof that the child's playing is important. The caretaker authorizes the child. He or she demonstrates with a "Wow!" that the child has done something important in the world.

While this account is focused on the life of a child, it isn't unreasonable to claim that this process of *presentist* recognition, this process of affirmation in the presence of an other, continues throughout adult life. Such a process is certainly at work when one is faced with the authority of a teacher. When we look to a teacher for affirmation of our learning, we are not unlike that child who excitedly reaches for a toy in anticipation that his caretaker will say, "Wow!" When a runner runs her hardest under the watchful eye of coach Hoffman, will she not look to that coach for a sign of affirmation? Will she not want to know that the coach shares her feeling of accomplishment? In the presence of a teacher, a student experiences the other's authority, the other's recognition for the learning she has done. In the presence of a teacher, the student gains a shared sense of experience. And, "The sense of shared feeling about the undertaking [or, the learning] is not only a reassurance, but is, itself, a source of pleasurable connection."[5] That is to say, the presence of an other is more full than the presence of oneself alone. In the presence of an other, one gains recognition from an authority figure that one cannot attain on one's own.

But this experience of presence with an other can also be described as the beginning of non-presence. Yes, recognition by an authority figure is initially dependent upon an authority who is actually *there*. But, this initial act of being affirmed in the flesh for a swift run or a subtle interpretation of a literary passage, such an initial act will certainly be followed by further efforts at running, further efforts at reading, further efforts when the teacher is no longer present. And, during such times of non-presence, is it not the case that the other is still with us to some extent? Is it not the case that the authority figure lingers as a powerful agent of affirmation, even at a time far removed from the actual experience under her watchful eye? The student is still bound with the teacher who has offered affirmation in the past, just as the child continues to be bound with his caregiver even into adulthood. The experience of presence with an other is already the beginning of non-presence with the other. For, when we are no longer in the physical presence of an authority figure, that authority figure still lingers in what Benjamin calls "inner space." Outward contact with the other always entails the beginning of an *inward contract* with the Other.

At this point it might seem easy to say that the case is closed, that the problem of the authoritative remnant is not such a problem after all. One might say at this point that the remnant is always at work because the unconscious is always at work. One might say that educational thought has been hamstrung by a metaphysics of presence because it has refused to sufficiently admit the pedagogical role the unconscious. But this is not my point at all.

My point here is not simply to restate a common psychological insight, the insight that one's relation to an authority figure becomes internalized in the form of unconscious bonds with him or her. My aim here is rather to unpack how the workings of such inner bonds might be more involved with educational interactions than is commonly acknowledged. For, it is not just that there is an educationally important remnant that lingers in the inner world of the student once the teacher is no longer present. In addition, the remnant plays a significant role within the *ongoing* process of education. The remnant, while indeed facilitating the presence of a non-presence when the student is out of reach of the teacher, is also an anchor point by which further interaction with the teacher will become meaningful. In other words, the remnant has a second role. The remnant actually affects the real experience of the student once he or she comes face to face with that teacher from whom she has been absent for some time.

I turn once again to the circuit of recognition to limn this second role. Following Benjamin, we should note that there are two main components to interhuman relations: the "intrapsychic," and the "intersubjective."[6] *Intrapsychic* life is the life of mental holdings, the life of the remnant. But intersubjective life is the real-life counterpart to the remnant. It is that part of experience that puts the remnant to the test. When one comes face to face with an authority figure, such face-to-face-ness serves as a foil to the isolated experience of the remnant, where one could formerly manipulate the authority figure, where the other used to be my own private other. Thus, a remnant is always the remnant of a specific other, an other who is likely to take one aback when intersubjective contact is reestablished. As such, there is always a give-and-take between the remnant, on the one hand, and fleshly contact with the other, on the other. Human experience is not primarily intrapsychic, as much psychoanalytic thought would have it. Nor is human experience based primarily on the interaction with the "real" authority figure, as so much presentist thought would have it. Human experience is a give and take between the remnant and the real.

Let us follow this present/absent theory of authority once again from the beginning, starting from a presentist conception, then moving to a version of the remnant, and then back again from the remnant to the real. When I come into contact with a teacher, I do so with a certain neediness. The teacher is important for my own growth as a person. I look to the teacher for recognition, for sustenance, for encouragement. I need the teacher to act as a mirror, reflecting who I am and who I am becoming. It is such an other, the teacher, who lets me know that my own actions are valuable, and that I am a person who has an affect on other people in this world. Yet at the same time, experiencing the authority figure's presence is bound to be unsettling. Indeed, the other is a separate "center of self," to borrow Benjamin's phrase.[7] The teacher as other is someone whom I do not control. Thus, while the teacher may offer me confidence and agency, she will doubtless shock me at some time. She will sometimes react in ways that I don't expect, sometimes in ways that do not offer me the recognition that I want. I will, after all, fail the authority figure's test from time to time. Thus, it is dangerous to depend wholly on the teacher. Such dependence will, at the end of the day, leave me tethered to an other whom I don't control. The teacher is a danger as well as a source of agency.

Vis-à-vis such a situation of danger and agency, the inner life of the remnant offers a buffer. When I leave the presence of the teacher, I am left with an inner conception of what the teacher has to offer me. This inner conception will be more under my control, more malleable to my needs, my wants, my autonomous actions. As Benjamin notes, "This 'inside' is the internal version of the safe transitional space (open space) that allows us to feel that our impulses come from within and so are authentically our own."[8] The remnant is under our control. The remnant is a version of authority that lets us replay the sort of recognition that we need from the other, even in the absence of that other. The inner life affords us an arena for play, for creativity, for experimentation, and for learning that is sheltered from the vicissitudes of the fleshly teacher. Under the watchful eyes of a teacher remnant, a teacher *whom I control*, I can practice my own ways of being, my own autonomous actions, without the threat of a teacher who might disappoint. In this way, the very nonpresence of the teacher is as central to the development of agency as the presence of that teacher. The remnant, cut from the same cloth as the real, functions as a prosthetic authority figure.

But as recognitive theory reminds us, the inner life contributes to agency only if it is ultimately tested in the real world. While the remnant is a safe space, one where I am in control, the remnant remains a space *of fantasy* unless it is tested against the real. Real agency cannot be fostered solely by remnants because agency is ultimately enacted in real life. In order for the teacher's recognition of me to count, she must have the real-life, presentist opportunity *not* to offer me recognition. In order for my agency to count, that agency must be tested in circumstances that could in fact end in disappointment. Thus, the remnant and the real exist in a symbiotic relationship. The inner life of the remnant cannot exist successfully on its own. An exclusively inner life leads to pathology, where playful imaginings of the remnant are never given a reality check, where the other is always a smiling face. Similarly, the intersubjective life cannot exist successfully on its own. A life experienced solely on the outside affords no zone of safety, no place where agency can be fostered without being constantly under threat, no place where the authority figure is not bound to surprise me *too much*. An exclusively outer life also leads to pathology, where submission to the whims of authority is the order of the day.

Think again of the thoughtful literary instruction of Professor Depuis, or the skilled coaching of Mr. Hoffman. While we described these teachers, at first, as a source of looming, beneficent presence, it is important now to amend that picture. On the one hand, yes, these teachers represent sources of inspiration, sources of educational agency, a warm cup of tea on a cold winter's day, if you will. The teacher, as a non-present, unconscious figure, continues to act as an active agent of motivation for his or her former student, *but not only because the teacher may have been an excellent teacher*. For, the teacher-as-remnant was once a teacher-in-the-flesh, a teacher who certainly had ups and downs of his or her own, who may not, in reality, have been the same inspiring figure that we now remember. Thus, the remnant serves a very important role in mitigating between, on the one hand, the active influence that a teacher has over his or her pupil, and, on the other, the safe space that is necessary to assimilate, to experiment with, and to make one's own the knowledge and abilities that the "real" teacher has to offer. The real teacher, by virtue of her role as an authority, always has the potential to influence his or her pupil *too much*, to nip agency in the bud, perhaps even by willful domination of her student. The remnant of authority acts as a buffer in times of non-presence. It enables students to effect a modicum of control over the teacher's authority. In the space of non-presence, the teacher is freeze-framed; the recognition that she offers can be invoked or disinvoked in order to decrease the threat of domination.

But let us think further about the remnant of authority and its real counterpart, about Professor Depuis and Mr. Hoffman as they were, but also about how they might be when they return. What is most educative may indeed *not* be the safe inner space afforded by the remnant. While the remnant may provide a mechanism for the agency of a student vis-à-vis an authority figure who is not present, isn't there also a sense in which education has already ended if the one-who-educates is once and for all relegated to a freeze-framed role? While it may be true that a student feels good about the remnant, that a student is eager to engage with the subject matter (Toni Morrison, running) associated with the smiling remnant, isn't it also true that the freeze-framed remnant has also lost the educative ability to challenge, to provoke, *to lead out* in the etymological sense of *educare*? It is at this point that I would say Professor Depuis and Mr. Hoffman should no longer be described as good teachers. Rather than still being effective teachers, they are, rather, set-in-stone objects in our memories, more monu/mental, if I can partake in this bit of punning, than they are educative.

In fact, what may be of more educational significance than the experience of the remnant is the symbiotic relation between the remnant and the real. Following the logic of recognition theory we should note that, while the remnant is a buffer to the real, being a buffer does not guarantee that the remnant contributes, on its own, to student agency. While the relation of non-presence with Professor Depuis is certainly a safer relation to have than the more unanticipatable relation that one has with her in the flesh; while the remnant of her "thoughtful guidance" may be a happy illusion of classroom experiences that were much more filled with tension, misrecognition, and domination than our unconscious chooses to recall; even so, a happy illusion is not necessarily a safe illusion in the long run. When the remnant of authority becomes the sole vehicle by which to gauge the extent to which one has become educated, the result is a solipsistic, inner-oriented educational experience that is dominated by private imaginings.

Consider cases where the remnant of authority tends to run rampant: Don't many of us know someone who always presents his or her educational reminiscences in glorious terms, but who, in a sort of performative contradiction, seems to be distinctly uneducated, decidedly unwise? For a student to *truly* learn from the lessons offered in the presence of Professor Depuis, the remnant of that teacher must be given a reality check. After one spends some time away from the presence of Professor Depuis, the real Professor Depuis must be encountered again in person in order for the student to gauge whether he can benefit from the real teacher in ways that are anything like the ways he benefited from her remnant. Without such a further encounter, the student's experience of the remnant may become tarnished by the nagging doubt that he or she might not be able to handle the fleshly experience that, ultimately, cannot be avoided since we are social beings. If a student stays solely in the realm of the authoritative remnant, then education stops.

EDUCATIONAL STOPOVERS:
BETWEEN THE REMNANT AND THE REAL

So I would ultimately like to argue for the interdependence of presence and non-presence when it comes to educational authority. It seems that education is necessarily influenced by instances of authoritative presence *as well as* by instances of authoritative non-presence. Why? Because the remnant is central to the real just as the real is central to the remnant. By this I don't mean that we should mysteriously know what our students are up to even when they are not in our presence. Nor do I mean that we should discount the significance of the time students spend *with* teachers.

What I mean, rather, is that we should pay more heed to the importance of educational stopovers, to those times when teachers and students leave each others' presence, and those times when they return to each other once again. Too often, these liminal moments are seen as unimportantly transitional, secondary to the times when students and teachers are actually in each other's presence, or, in more progressivist moments, secondary to the times that students are on their own, encountering what John Dewey calls "experience."[9] To put this another way, let's say that any consideration of the ends of education should also take into account the fact that education needs to have ends, many ends. It also needs to have many new beginnings. Authority should leave and then come back, leave and then come back. Education must have numerous ends and numerous beginnings if students and teachers are to take advantage of the give-and-take that is necessary between the remnant and the real.

In fact, it is important to note that this give-and-take between the remnant and the real is actually a very accurate description of day-to-day relations as they are practiced in our educational institutions. What I mean by this is that educational institutions have, for the most part, a certain rhythm. Students engage with teachers sometimes daily, sometimes weekly, and then there is time built in for them to be away from their teachers. As the logic of the remnant shows us, the time spent away from the teacher is more than a time for one to complete one's exercises. It is more than a time to complete one's reading. It is more than a cooling-off period away from the pressures of school. Time spent away from the teacher can also be an unconscious reenactment of the ways that one experiences authority in the flesh. And while the unconscious reenactment of the teacher's presence will be part of the student's inner world, a part of that over which the student has complete control, it is important for the growth of the educational relation that there be time together to augment inner experience with outer reality. The student must come once again into contact with the "real" authority figure in order that inner images do not come to dominate.

This particular way of construing the comings and goings (the "ends") of education casts a different light on the day-to-day rhythm of educational interactions with authority. The actions of the teacher are important, yes. But, it is in the oscillation between presence and non-presence, and back again, where such actions gain their significance. Is it not interesting that so much educational research treats the school as a petri dish of presence, while the actual rhythm of education so clearly enacts a back-and-forth between the remnant and the real? Especially when it comes to the matter of authority, the school should not be treated as a petri dish of presence.

Of course, there is a paradox that is certainly present (and certainly also non-present) when we delve into the role of the remnant and the real of educational authority. *The paradox, clearly stated, is this*: successful educational authority always depends upon presence *and* absence. Thus, one finds real difficulties when one tries to describe "successful" authority. For, to describe successful educational authority, one can only describe that which is describable, that which is *present*. So, just when one is in a position to describe an instance of "successful" authority, just then, it may be that authority is no longer successful precisely because it has become solely a matter of presence. At the moment when authority is present, freeze-framed, and describable, the educative role of authority may have already passed.

One might thus wonder if my fond reminiscence of Professor Depuis is not actually more of a testament to the fact that she no longer has a role in educating me than it is a testament to what she once had to offer me as an educator. Such a reminiscence leaves me with a profound remnant, but with little in the way of a reality check. After a consideration of the give-and-take between authority's absence and its presence, I must wonder if a *truly great teacher* isn't rather one who has refused to make a lasting impression on us. Or at the very least, isn't she one who is remembered as a bit enigmatic? Isn't she one who continues to be troublesome because unexpected? Isn't she one who continues to force an engagement with the real rather than a fond recalling of the ideal?

PRESENCE AND ABSENCE,
THE SPOKEN AND THE WRITTEN

A few years ago, I was speaking to a colleague about a philosophy conference that we were both going to attend. She mentioned how happy she was that there were to be no simultaneous presentation sessions. She was happy that everyone would be present to listen to everyone else's papers. She was pleased that papers were not to be given in different rooms at the same time because, she said, "this way, everyone will be able to listen, and perhaps respond, to every paper." I think her observation goes right to the heart of an important relational notion that many people hold dear. For many, it is very important to have face-to-face dialogue instead of simply reading the hard copy. Colleagues come together in order to learn. We come together to see each other. We come together to hug or shake hands. All of this is facilitated by the shared experience of living dialogue.

My colleague's comment is about presence and absence. It is also about dialogue versus reading. In many people's eyes, dialogue is how people become most *present* to one another. The question I pursue in the pages that follow in this chapter is this: What is the role of speaking, as opposed to the role of reading, in the authority relation? I pursue this question to add nuance to a few themes that I have already been looking into in the previous pages of this study. First, I have already started an investigation into the place of texts within the relation of authority. That investigation was based mainly on curricular texts that have been written by people *other* than the teacher. This account of written texts will expand that initial investigation and open it up to texts and other communiqués that are written by the teacher herself. Second, I have already made the claim that a relational understanding of language is central to a relational understanding of authority. Thus, what follows will augment the performative account of communication that I have already offered, showing how language works, within the performance of an authority relation, to negotiate the presence and absence of speakers and listeners. What follows is based on an account of authority in the realm of academia. However, I am confident that what is examined here should be clearly applicable to the authority relation as it occurs in many educational settings.

To address the question of speaking and writing in the authority relation, I will look into two more versions of the role that language plays in human relations. These two understandings of language augment the performative account described earlier without falling back into the sender-receiver model that we should rightly reject. The first version derives from the phenomenological work of Maurice Merleau-Ponty. I will detail Merleau-Ponty's account of language and relationality, but show that it has several limitations. Then, I will pick up on some of the work done in the previous pages by examining the psychoanalytic perspective on speech provided by Jessica Benjamin's intersubjective psychoanalysis. Intersubjective psychoanalysis highlights the importance of present/absent interaction. By looking into Benjamin's theory of language, I will show that her viewpoint fills in some important gaps in what I call Merleau-Ponty's "traditional" view of speech. Ultimately, I will come back to my colleague's observation on listening to one another, as opposed to simply reading each other's papers, at conferences. Her observation was quite correct: we *are* well met at conferences such as the one we both attended. Sometimes hard copies simply will not do. The living relation of authority is most appropriately brought alive through the performative enactment that occurs via the living word.

THE PROBLEM OF INTERSUBJECTIVITY

Before jumping right into language, though, let us start with the more general philosophical "problem of intersubjectivity." Intersubjectivity has been the concern of a wide range of philosophers who have wanted to know how one subject recognizes another subject. In phenomenological terms, the question is posed like this: If the other is constituted within one's own ego, then how can we account for the specificity of the other? How can I constitute an other who is self-constituting? Won't the other's self-constituting just be a version of my own self-constituting? Is there a way to understand the experience of relationality other than merely saying, "I really don't know the other; all I know is my own version of the other"?

Edmund Husserl, for example, addresses the problem of inter-subjectivity in his *Cartesian Mediations.*[10] There, he employs the notion of "pairing" to show how the ego attains intersubjectivity. Pairing is a developmental answer to the predicament of intersubjectivity. As Husserl explains, pairing happens early in the ego's development, and it sets the stage for intersubjectivity later in life. The mother (or whoever the nurturer is) makes available the child's first "apperceptive" experience of otherness.[11] In words that are not as phenomenologically technical, we might say that the mother, or caretaker, is vaguely experienced both as other and as part of the ego. According to Husserl, the two members of this pair "found phenomenologically a unity of similarity and thus are always constituted precisely as a pair."[12] This is before the ego constitutes itself as a separate ego. Then, even after self-constitution, the ego continues to constitute others by analogy to the self-mother pair. The other is like the mother, who was, and still is, like me. The more mature, self-consituting ego understands others to be self-constituting also. A mature other can be self-constituting because others can be like me—just as the mother was once like me.

Some followers of Husserl are not sure that the origin of intersubjectivity can be situated at the primordial stage, just before self-constitution of the ego. Even if the self-other analogy begins early on, the problem of solipsism ensues later. Later on, when the self-constituting other is recognized to be just like me, then hasn't her self-constituting turned out to be a version of my own self-constituting? Pairing may have started *before* self-constituting, but it still ends up there. A developed ego loses the *vague* perception of pairing. However, its pairing now happens within the realm of self-constitution—which leads us back to the original predicament of intersubjectivity. As Maurice Merleau-Ponty reminds us, "To be conscious is to constitute, so that I cannot be conscious of another person, since that would involve constituting him as constituting."[13] Husserl does not get past the problem of solipsism.

MERLEAU-PONTY'S TRADITIONAL VIEW OF RELATIONAL LANGUAGE

Following up on his objection to Husserl's developmental, "pairing" explanation of intersubjectivity, Merleau-Ponty looks to language. He argues that language provides the bedrock of intersubjectivity. In his essay entitled "The Phenomenology of Language," Merleau-Ponty shows how language provides a medium for intersubjectivity.[14] I will call his conception the "traditional" view of intersubjective language. The traditional view points out two dimensions of language.[15] The first dimension is *not* intersubjective: language forms a set of cultural signifiers that are commonly understood among people who share that language. In this dimension, a word is understood to be an object, just like a stone or a table. Just as we share some understanding of what an object such as a stone is, we also share some understanding of what a word is, what it means. This first dimension of language is not properly intersubjective because, according to the phenomenological view, intersubjectivity means recognizing another subject, another self. Just because two subjects recognize a common object in language, that does not necessarily mean that they recognize *each other*. Intersubjectivity is not guaranteed just because two people recognize common objects or share common meanings.

The second dimension of language brings us into the realm of intersubjectivity. It does so as follows: When I speak, I give to language the unique quality of my intended meaning. And when an other speaks, she also gives to language the unique quality of her intended meaning. In this second dimension, language is no longer an object in the sense that a stone is an object. Instead, language is a uniquely *linguistic* object insofar as it lets an other demonstrate her subjectivity. A Merleau-Ponty explains, spoken language serves to "reverse my ordinary relationship to objects and give certain ones of them the value of subjects."[16] If an other picks up a stone, the stone remains the same stone just as it would remain the same stone if I (as opposed to the other) were to pick it up. When the other picks up a stone, that picking-up does not convince me that an other's consciousness is different from my own. When an other speaks, though, she invests language with a unique meaning that I could not replicate. It is as if she has changed the stone's stoneness in a way that I could never have done. Through using language, the other convinces me of her specific subjectivity. Language, in its second dimension, is thus a vehicle for intersubjectivity, for relation.

While this traditional view of language and intersubjectivity is appealing, I would like to point out several of its limitations. First of all, this view of language is not longitudinal, to borrow a term from the social sciences. The traditional view does not explain why we keep speaking with others over a long period of time. What I mean is, If the ego recognized the specificity of an other once, why would one keep speaking with the other? In terms of the comment made by my colleague with regard to our conference, if I have already been to one of someone's presentations, why not just read the hard copy of that person's thoughts from then on? Or in terms of a love relationship, should I quit speaking with my partner in person just because we have come to an intersubjective realization of each other's consciousnesses? Speaking seems to be an ongoing project, but why? The traditional view of intersubjective language does not answer this question.

Second, the traditional view of language does not account for the speaker behind the speech. If speech is a *vehicle* for intersubjectivity, then there is still a unique subject *behind* the speech that needs to be dealt with. Speech may help us to recognize the specificity of another subject, but what if I have problems with that other subject? What if that other subject is threatening to me? In the traditional view of intersubjective speech, it seems that speech is a means for establishing a *positive* relation with the other; speech leads to empathy. Does speech have any function when the other is someone I do *not* want to recognize? To return again to the experience of attending a conference and to listening to papers, is there some reason to speak with a presenter whose views I loathe?

A third limitation follows directly from the second. What if the subject behind the speech is *too* appealing? What if an other's unique subjectivity threatens to engulf my own uniqueness? Following the traditional view, it seems that speech serves to clarify the specificity of the other, and thus to intensify the other's charm. In the case of one who attends a conference, why would I speak with an other who threatens to overshadow me with the appeal of her views, with the logic of her arguments?

And because I want ultimately to relate an intersubjective theory of language to the problem of relational authority, let me translate these three objections into terms that speak to the communication that takes place with an authority figure. If language acts according to this traditional intersubjective model, why, once I have ascertained the authoritative status of the person with whom I speak, would I ever need to listen to such an authority figure again? Couldn't I just accept, after that initial ascertainment, that every other thing I hear from, or about, that person is equally authoritative? Would authority ever need to be enacted more than once between two people? Or, if language does serve to establish a relational understanding of an authority figure, mightn't my potential fear of an other be an inordinate deterrent to communication in cases where I guess, beforehand, that the other has the potential to dominate me? Or conversely, following my third objection to the traditional view, mightn't language be the royal road to domination? Mightn't communication with an authority figure turn out to be too convincing, too enticing, to the point where one abandons one's own stance through engaging in the relation of authority?

I sense that Merleau-Ponty is quite justified in claiming that language is a key element for attaining intersubjectivity, for recognizing an other as a subject in her own right. And, I am quite sure that the traditional view goes much farther toward establishing language's intersubjective role than the more common sender-receiver understanding of communication. However, recent work in intersubjective psychoanalysis offers a more helpful view of language's intersubjective role. Specifically, intersubjective psychoanalysis sheds light on the three limitations of the traditional view that I have described. It also highlights the importance of everyday dialogue at a conference such as the one I have been referring to.

LANGUAGE AND THE REMNANT

Intersubjectivity in psychoanalytic discourse, it will be recalled, relies upon a distinction between *intrapsychic* space and *intersubjective* space. Defining the term *intersubjectivity*, Benjamin says that it "refers to that zone of experience in which the other is not merely the object of the ego's need/drive or cognition/perception but has a separate and equivalent center of self."[17] This distinction—between the other recognized as object and the other recognized as subject—is the distinction between the intrapsychic and the intersubjective. Whereas intrapsychic space involves internal, psychic manipulation of the other, intersubjective space involves recognition of the other as a subject with agency. According to Benjamin, the other always remains an object if she remains only in the psychic realm. Intersubjectivity ensues when we confront the other "out there in the real world," on his or her own terms.

It is easy to see the essential similarity between the phenomenological version of intersubjectivity, *à la* Husserl, and the psychoanalytic version. For each version, intersubjectivity consists in recognizing the other *as autonomous subject*. There is, however, a difference in how objects are construed by these two versions. In the psychoanalytic view, the other-as-object is manipulated in intrapsychic space, while the other-as-subject resides "out there in the real world." In the phenomenological view, though, the other-as-object does not reside in a *different* space than the other-as-subject. In this latter view, they both reside in the same world of "intended" others. Another difference that characterizes the psychoanalytic view is that it does not consider intersubjectivity to be an automatic state of human consciousness. Instead, intersubjectivity is an achievement. We sometimes refuse intersubjectivity, or intersubjectivity is avoided because it is unbearable. Since confronting the other as a subject with agency can be threatening, often it is more comfortable to experience the other as an object under our control. In such cases, we disregard the other-as-subject and represent him as an object in the psyche.

Because of this last difference, a psychoanalytic understanding of intersubjectivity suggests that, often, the self becomes swollen with objectifying representations of the other. Unfortunately, if our relation to the other resides mainly in intrapsychic space, then the self will experience a sudden crisis when faced with an other who proves to be a subject with agency. In this case, if the other acts in an unanticipated way, I will feel *doubly* threatened because I do not anticipate its agency. In the face of this double threat, I will feel *my own* subjectivity diminished. In order to avoid this sudden threat, in order to be an autonomous subject in my own right, I must accept that intrapsychic representations of the other are *not* equivalent to the autonomous other "out there in the real world." I can only be an autonomous subject if I can negotiate between the intrapsychic realm and the intersubjective realm.

This is where language comes to play a different role than the one suggested by Merleau-Ponty. Language facilitates the move between intrapsychic space and intersubjective space.[18] Language makes use of symbols.[19] As such, it enables us to practice going from reality to symbol, and from symbol to reality, over and over. This oscillation between symbol and reality happens because language itself is a way to negotiate between the intrapsychic and the intersubjective realms. That is to say, just as the other can be either intrapsychically constructed, or, can be recognized as an actual, living subject; so, too, can language freeze-frame thoughts and actions and thus offer a dual status for people with whom we come into contact. Language works within a system that can offer steadfast words to substitute for less steadfast living beings. Take for example the word, *Grandma*. This word offers a steadfast, freeze-framed sign of the living woman who is one's grandmother. Language negotiates between objects in the outside world and our inside representations of those objects. Language "constitutes a space of fluctuating convergence and divergence between inner and outer," to borrow the words of Benjamin.[20]

Let me offer an example, from my own life, of this outside/inside use of language. My daughter, Olivia, when she was two years old, was just at the point of entering the realm of language. At that point, her use of language was limited, although it was already very helpful to her. For example, sometimes she and I would visit her grandparents even though we did not spend a lot of time around them on a daily basis. Nevertheless, even when Olivia was away from her grandparents, she was able to use language to conjure up images of them that would bring a smile to her face. For instance, when I would speak to Olivia of a nearby zoo that we had visited together with her grandparents, a smile would come to her face as she would say, "Grandma Grandpa zoo." "Yes," I would tell her, "Grandma and Grandpa were at the zoo with us." Even before Olivia had stepped completely into language, she could use language as a system to negotiate between what was present and what was absent. She could use language to negotiate between inner representations of her grandparents and outer experiences with them in real life.

According to Benjamin's view—the view that language provides a symbolic space for play, for practicing the transition from intersubjective to the intrapsychic, and back again—Olivia's evocation of her grandparents enables her to do two things: First, it enables her to let go of her grandparents, allowing them to be independent subjects who come and go as they please. In other words, Olivia can accept the departure of her grandparents because she has words that evoke their presence even in their absence. Conjuring up the image of her grandparents by saying their names, Olivia can smile even though they are not under her direct control. This first use of language allows her to practice moving from the intersubjective realm to the intrapsychic realm as she changes Grandma and Grandpa into intrapsychic representations. Second, language enables her to negotiate the return of Grandma and Grandpa when she finally sees them again. When they return, Olivia will be reminded that her intrapsychic image of Grandpa and Grandma—the picture in her mind that their names evoke—is, perhaps, not the same as their physical presence. Whereas their images can be evoked almost at will, Grandpa and Grandma really only come back when they want to. Upon their return, she will once again be reminded that they are autonomous subjects. This second use of language helps her to move from intrapsychic space to intersubjectivity.

Another important role of language between subjects is the role of mediation.[21] This is not the simple role of "softening reality" as some would have it who unthinkingly say, "Sticks and stones can break my bones but words can never hurt me." Rather, it is the complex role of negotiating the tension between inner and outer life. For example, if I am in face-to-face contact with an other, I may feel threatened by his or her aggression. I may feel overwhelmed by the force of his or her physical presence, or I may feel overwhelmed by the force of his or her argument. Language's symbolization enables me to create a safe haven even during such an onslaught of the other. Let us say that I have stage fright just before speaking with a person whose ideas and writings I have long revered. I can use strategies of linguistic symbolization to keep myself fortified, to temper the anxiety that threatens to overcome my very being. I may say to myself, "She is just like any other person. She is made of flesh and blood like my daughter, and I am never afraid to interact with my daughter." In this way, the symbolic quality of language enables one to mediate the incursion of an other onto the agency of self. It is not that language *never* allows the other to affect the self. If the other could not affect the self, then the other would not be an agentive subject, and intersubjectivity would cease. It is, rather, that language enables the self to be affected without being lost.

As the above examples show, language does work in the realm of the subject/object pair, in the ongoing relational problem of how subjects come to recognize others as more than mere objects. Intersubjectivity, as it gets elaborated in the psychoanalytic tradition, always happens in juxtaposition to intrapsychic activity. That is to say, there is never pure intersubjectivity nor is there pure intrapsychic life. There is only oscillation between the two. Similarly, human language exists in oscillation between the symbolic and the real. Language is neither pure symbol nor is it pure object. Rather, language acts in ways that parallel the inner/outer split. And as long as language has referents, language will be integral to intersubjectivity.

BETWEEN THE PAPER AND THE WORD

What has all this to do with education? With authority? In education, there is often a choice to be made between absence and presence. It takes the form of a choice between the paper and the word. In education, one must constantly negotiate between written pronouncements and living dialogue. When a student reads what a teacher has written, there is absence. When a student talks with a teacher, there is presence.

Students submit essays, term papers, written tests, written exams, as well as other forms of written texts that are read by teachers. Teachers give out notes. They deliver prepared lectures. They offer students written evaluations. They hand out opinion papers and essays that they themselves have written. They give out grades. All of these are set-in-stone forms of communication. These documents and pronouncements are severely limiting if they are not accompanied by dialogue. Dialogue is central to the educational relation. The relation will certainly entail hard copies, but it should utilize more fluid aspects of communication, too. In this way, the teachers with whom students interact have a chance to return with unexpectedness, with surprise.

In classrooms, we have missed something very important if we overfocus on the written documents that are exchanged between student and teacher. Yes, it may be the case that texts are thoughtfully submitted, thoughtfully critiqued, thoughtfully graded and assessed. Yes, it may be the case that student and teacher are "happy" that an even-handed relation of authority has been enacted through such exchanges of text. However, it must be remembered that fully functioning authority depends upon the dynamic interchange between the written and the spoken. This happens just as every relation depends upon the dynamic interchange between the remnant and the real. Dialogue about what has been written is as important as the physical return of a teacher who has been absent. The speaking teacher is always a "supplement" to what has been written.

But what is the use of dialogue if a teacher threatens to overwhelm me with his or her allure? As I have tried to show earlier, the psychic life of language actually helps to *mediate* between self and other. Speaking with an other provides a symbolic space for interaction that can temper the aggression of an other toward the self. If I speak with someone whose otherness threatens to engulf me, then the words we exchange can become objects for my manipulation. Using the symbolic, intrapsychic qualities of language, I can achieve a certain distance from the other, a distance that helps to attenuate the onslaught of that other. In cases where the other is threatening, the linguistic distance of dialogue can help me to keep my own subjectivity intact. So while it might seem at first glance that I should *not* speak with an other who might be threatening to me, in fact, language serves to help us through those times when we are about to be engulfed by another person's ideas, by another person's presence. Dialogue can serve to de-ossify the seemingly overwhelming quality of an other's ideas.

When student and teacher come together, the relational nature of language makes space for agency. Dialogue between student and teacher can offer something much different than what the student had suspected was "behind the door." To be engaged in dialogue is not simply to be exposed in an unadulterated manner to the perspectives, ideas, and opinions of another person. Quite the contrary, dialogue may serve to mitigate some elements of the authority relation that might be quite rigid without such dialogue. As counterintuitive as this may seem, please consider the following: when the other threatens to engulf me with his rigid opinions; when the other seems to have me in an authoritative relation where I feel squelched—just then it may be that I can use dialogue with the other to my benefit, to the enhancement of my own capacity.

And what about instances when the other seems repulsive? It might seem as if there is little reason to speak with a person whose written viewpoints I simply cannot stand. Such a rejection of dialogue with a loathsome other is based on the premise that dialogue will only serve to accentuate an other's loathsomeness. Actually, it is not necessarily the case that the "real" other is as anticipatable as the carved-in-stone written other. Yes, I may dislike the substance of a person's writings. However, there is always a difference between the fleshly author and that which he or she writes. There will always be a *dis*continuity between authorship and the spoken word. The spoken word is a supplement to the written word in both senses of "supplementarity." The spoken will not only have natural connections to the written word, but it will have post-natural additions to the written word too. There is little reason to think that the author's fleshly interaction with me will be synonymous with her text's influence on me. For, the intersubjective nature of language is such that dialogue opens up new symbolic qualities that depend upon the relation between speakers as much as they depend upon what the author has written in the past.

So it is not necessarily the case that the authority that gets enacted between teacher and student in dialogue will be the same as the authority that has been enacted by means of teacherly pronouncements. If a student decides, beforehand, that a teacher's objectionable lecture, or the objectionable comments that a teacher makes on a student's work, will be synonymous with the authority that gets enacted through conversation with that same teacher, this is a mistake. Dialogue between student and teacher itself opens up new vistas that may not be as loathsome as one might anticipate.

Once again, what I am trying to say is this: there is a dynamic interaction between teacher pronouncements, on the one hand, and student-teacher dialogue, on the other, that closely parallels the dynamic between absence and presence. It may be that the very antidote to the loathsomeness of the other comes from an experience that might at first glance be foreshadowed as an experience even more loathsome. It may be that talking with the other is less objectionable, and more agentive, than could ever have been imagined from a distance where distilled pronouncements seem to rule the day.

THE SIGNIFICANCE OF BOTH ABSENCE AND PRESENCE

For some, this chapter may seem inconclusive. It may seem at this point that I am advocating the benefits of *both* presence *and* absence. It may seem that there is no way to decide whether the authority relation gets enacted most prominently when there is presence, or most prominently when there is absence. In fact, *there is no way* to decide. I began this chapter by noting that current understandings of authority focus too much on presence. They certainly do. So, if it has accomplished anything, this chapter has served to make the reader aware of the place of absence within the authority relation. Please note, though, that I do not claim that there is any clear-cut way to decide *which* is more significant to the authority relation, presence or absence. What I have attempted to show is, first, that absence is significant, and second, that the real and the remnant are symbiotically related, each living off of the other.

Another way of stating this is to say that there is no "behind the door" to presence and absence. There is no preordained essence to either one. Rather, presence and absence (or, alternatively, authority in dialogue and authority that has been distilled into written pronouncements) are significant to the extent that they are related to each other. Each gains its educational import in its performance, rather than behind the door. Hence the ongoing nature of both presence and absence. The nature of presence and absence in the authority relation is always *to be* worked out.

Acknowledging presence and absence yields new insight into the workings of student agency vis-à-vis their teachers. Once we know that the impact of the authority relation depends upon the dynamic interaction between presence and absence, we also know that there is plenty of wiggle room for students to configure their relationships to authority *even when teachers are not around.* Thus, students should not only be encouraged to gain voice and confidence when they speak with teachers face to face. They should also be encouraged to gain the agency when they experience the remnants of teachers. This can happen as student rethink the freeze-framed effects of teachers who have made their impact through marks, through written communications, and through teacherly lectures. Cognizance of the remnant, and of its interaction with the real, reminds us that what one does with educational authority on one's own is just as important as how one experiences that authority in the flesh. Such cognizance reminds us that students have much control over the effects of educational authority.

Educators should make it clear to students that students have power to treat authority as they see fit. There is a particular opportunity to do so when authority figures are not around. The relation between presence and absence is one that should depend, to a large extent, upon the actions of students. As a student, how I relate to a Professor Depuis, to a coach Hoffman, or to a history teacher such as Julie's, is to a large extent under my own control, at least when such figures of authority are not around. And even when such authority figures do come back into the picture, I have a chance, myself, to alter the effect that their return has on me. For, the return of an authority figure can depend greatly on my stance toward him or her while he or she was away. The wiggle room between presence and absence affords great space for student agency.

It is the more general matter of student agency vis-à-vis authority that will be the subject of the next chapter. There, I will outline some of the ways that we might encourage students to be active participants in the authority relation. I will look into how students can "use" the relation of authority to their benefit. I will look into how students might "use" their teachers in ways that are agentive. In addition, I will examine how students can use *larger* forces of authority to their benefit, these forces being: the force of natural inclination, the force of acculturation, and the force of tradition.

CHAPTER 4

When Faced With Authority

Let us now look into the ways that we might orient ourselves toward authority. For, if authority is a relation, then it is not enough to say how authority operates. Nor is it enough to say which kinds of authority (non-present as well as present, textual as well as spoken) are involved in the authority relation. We must also ask what role we have to play when we are faced with authority. In the face of authority, what do we *do*? What might students do?

There are at least two ways to approach how we orient ourselves toward authority. First, we can think about how we face an other who is in authority. We can think about how we treat that other. Second, we can think about how we face authority when authority is bigger than an other, when authority is a societal force or a cultural tradition. We can consider when authority is a larger entity, rather than being a *specific* other. Of course how one orients oneself toward an other in authority, and how one orients oneself toward larger societal forces— these are immense topics, each one of them. In this chapter, I want to bite off just a small nibble from each of these immense topics. With regard to the other who is in authority, I will describe the benefits of "using" authority figures to our educational advantage. This "using" I will call "pragmatic intersubjectivity." With regard to how one treats oneself when facing larger forces of authority, I will explain some of the educational benefits of tending to one's own agency in such circumstances. To do this, I will be drawing upon the philosophical tradition of "self-fashioning."[1]

PRAGMATIC INTERSUBJECTIVITY,
OR, JUST USING TEACHERS

Pragmatism has long held sway in educational thought, especially in North America. While the "consequences of pragmatism" in education are many, one central tenet seems to emerge as influential again and again.[2] Here I am referring to the pragmatist notion of making all educational ends into means for further educational ends.[3] Such pragmatism gains purchase in educational thought because education is, after all, an ever-growing, never-ending project where curricular achievements lead to further curricular achievements. To make ends into means into further ends just keeps the ball rolling in a very educational sort of way. As John Dewey put it, "[T]he central problem of an education based upon experience is to select the kind of present experiences that live fruitfully and creatively in subsequent experiences."[4]

Of course, this tenet of pragmatism does not really apply to *people*. To my knowledge, Dewey never went so far as to say that people should use other people. He never said that it would be all right to turn a person into a means to a further end. In this way, John Dewey follows Immanuel Kant's moral dictum that every rational creature must be treated as an end in himself. Kant condemns the use of others. His condemnation is enmeshed with his understanding of autonomous selfhood, and with the dignity of such selfhood. As Kant puts it, "Man and, in general, every rational being exists as an end in himself and not merely as a means to be arbitrarily used by this or that will. . . . This principle . . . of every rational creature as an end in itself is the supreme limiting condition on freedom.[5] And Dewey toes a good, Kantian, moral line. He leaves *people* out of his pragmatism.

But let us be immoral for a bit. Let us bring people into the pragmatist picture. Let us bring students and teachers into this picture just for the sake of argument. I want to make the case that Dewey *should have* embraced pragmatism all the way down to the personal level. I want to suggest that, at least in the case of students and teachers, there should be some using going on. In particular, students should be using their teachers as means to further ends. Such a move of making human beings into means to further ends, of making teachers into means for the further ends of students, of going against Kant's categorical imperative, we might call "pragmatic intersubjectivity." Or, we might call it *just using people* in education.

Let us be immoral by arguing against the morality of Kant. Why might it be okay for one person to use another? Why might it be all right for one *not* in authority to use one who *is* in authority? Why should we *not* follow Kant's moral imperative? Well, from the standpoint of relational authority, Kant's order not to use another is, quite simply, impossible to follow! When it comes to the authority relation, Kant makes a faulty assumption to begin with. He assumes that the self is autonomous in its most "mature" state. In his response to the question, "What is Enlightenment?" Kant encourages each person to use his or her own authority in his or her own way. "Have the courage to use the authority of your own reason," Kant exhorts.[6] He assumes that human beings are fundamentally autonomous, and thus he imagines that how we relate to authority must honor the autonomy within each of us. Well, when it comes to the relation of authority, Kant picks the pan up by the wrong handle. I say this because once one realizes (contra Kant) that human beings are relational vis-à-vis authority, then relation, whether it be a dependency on others, or whether it be an instrumental use of others, is *not* something that we can simply choose to avoid. The moral pan should rather be picked up by its intersubjective handle.

Unlike Kant, we should take as a given that human beings exist in relation, and that the only optional matter is *how* we engage with another person. While Kant envisions an authority that one can engage with alone, we should envision the relation of authority as one wherein we *inevitably* use one another, at least to some extent. As I have been trying to argue throughout this work, human beings are always *already* relational, especially when authority is at play.

USING THE OTHER: NIETZSCHE, FOUCAULT, WINNICOTT

When we go against Kant, it may, at first blush, seem a bit immoral. But we are in good company. There is good philosophical grounding for the concept of pragmatic intersubjectivity. For example, Friedrich Nietzsche has responded to Kant's use-aversion with the bold statement that " 'autonomous' and 'moral' are mutually exlusive."[7] Nietzsche turns the Kantian moral imperative on its head. He does so by showing how moral decisions are always imbedded in a moral calculus that is already intersubjective. For Nietzsche, a person's moral decision is not something that is decided upon by the autonomous individual and then carried out in the fashion that the autonomous individual sees fit. A moral act is not carried out solely by the intention of the autonomous actor. On one's own, it is not actually possible to choose what is right or what is wrong. Rather, what is "right" or "good" is always already involved in a moral calculus that has been begun before the human actor has even considered making a moral choice. For Nietzsche, moral goods are always saturated with significance because of human obligations and human power struggles that have taken place in the past.

So in his famous example of early Christian morality, Nietzsche argues that some "moral" habits such as abstinence and moderation were deemed "moral" not out of autonomous free choice.[8] They were deemed "moral" only because they were forced on the early Christians by the ruling class. Under pressure from the other, Nietzsche maintains, one makes a virtue out of necessity. Moral decisions derive from intersubjective experience rather than from the free intentions of autonomous selves. Or to repeat his bold claim, " 'autonomous' and 'moral' are mutually exlusive."[9]

To put Nietzsche's observations in terms of means and ends, we can say that other people are *already* being used as means when we consider how to live well. Why? Because moral acts take place in the intersubjective realm. In stark contrast to Kant's aversion to using people, Nietzsche reminds us that somebody is going to be used in a certain way when we decide how best to act. Moral decisions are made possible precisely because somebody has been, or somebody will be, used. Systems of moral thought, even such large systems as Christianity, are always already predicated upon people being used.

We are also in the company of Michel Foucault. Foucault pushes Nietzsche's thought along. He demonstrates that it is not only the moral realm that is based on using others. More than that, all human subjectivity is born out of such relations. Human flourishing itself is a matter of subjection. For Foucault too, the Kantian ideal of human autonomy is a mistaken one. The telos of human selfhood is not that of becoming autonomous and staying autonomous. Instead, human selfhood always owes its existence to various cultural practices of dependency upon others. The self is situated by bio-power, by the power of surveillance, by confessional techniques, by epistemic regimes, by governmental hierarchies, etc.[10] For Foucault, human selfhood lives and breathes through processes of subjection. It is not that the self arrives on the scene first, and is then fettered by the power of others. Nor is it that the self is first indebted to the power of others and then proceeds to free itself from power little by little. Instead, the power of others constitutes the self to begin with, and it continues to form who the self is as time progresses. Power creates the self *and* fetters the self, doing both at the same time. For Foucault, the self is "the product of the relation of power."[11] As such, the only way for the human being to flourish is for him or her to work *within* the various relations of power.

To look ahead for a moment, we might say that the student's experience at school is one of those subjectifying processes that Foucault claims are central to human subjectivity. For Foucault, being a subject means being subjectified, and being a subject at school means being subjectified at school. Now, what this means for the student is that the only way to obtain agency in a place such as school is to engage with the subjectifying processes already at work. It is only possible to flourish by means of using the power-laden tools at hand. What I want to suggest in this chapter is that one of the subjectifying processes at school is the teacher-student relationship. Interaction with the teacher is one of those educational sites where student subjectivity is constituted. As such, one way for student flourishing to occur is through the strategic use of that site. Using teachers is one way to attain agency within the subjectifying processes of schooling.

D. W. Winnicott is keeping us company as well. Winnicott assails Kant from a psychoanalytic standpoint.[12] His insights not only bolster the "immoral" stance that I am putting forth here, but they provide a very practical way to think about how students might use authority in educational settings. For Winnicott, human agency is formed against the backdrop of using other people. As the child develops a sense of self, he or she does so by experimenting with the absence and presence of a primary caregiver. The child needs the presence of a caregiver in order to have a space that is safe for experimentation, creativity, and acquisition of new skills. She needs someone to fall back on when things fail. Yet the child also needs the absence of a caregiver insofar as she must be able to experiment, to create, and to acquire new skills *on her own*. The child needs spaces where the caregiver is there, but the child also needs spaces where the caregiver is not there. In order to establish these sorts of spaces, the child must sometimes call her caregiver to her side. At other times, she must banish the caregiver from her sight so that she can test what she can do alone. In both of these circumstances, the child must "use" the other in order to set the stage for growth. The child must manipulate the presence of an other so that the other is around sometimes and not around at others. The child must call on the other sometimes. At other times she must either implicitly or explicitly ask the other to leave. So even though the young child is in the process of establishing her own autonomy, this process includes an other. It includes the use of an other.

And as Winnicott points out, this practice of using others is not just a childhood matter. Throughout life, and in many different arenas, agency is *not* gained in a passive, nor in an isolated, way. It is through the active "use" of others that one flourishes. When we "use" other people, we call them to our sides or we banish them from our midst. And we must do so in an active way. If the other seeps in and out of our presence on her own volition, then *she* has control over how I can gain agency. It is only through *my own* use of others that I can create the circumstances where I am both dependent on, yet independent of, another person who serves as my guide.

So we need to use others in order to gain agency. Of course, this is not the end of the story. After all, not all people will let themselves be used. Not every person I meet will agree to both be at my beck and call and to be absent when I see fit. There must be a *relation* at work between the person who sometimes needs an other, and an other who accepts the challenge of being around at those particular times. For this other who is willing to be around, Winnicott introduces a concept that is very important for us, educationally speaking. It is the concept of the "good enough" mother. The good enough mother is the object of use. She is the person who avails herself to be used by another. She is the person who understands that another person needs her to be present at times and absent at others. If I am a good enough mother, I understand that my presence and absence are central to the autonomy, creativity, and thoughtfulness of the other. I understand that being around may not always be easy. For example, sometimes the other will try to "destroy" me.[13] Sometimes the other will try to banish me from his or her presence. And at such times, I may have a desire to leave the other for good. But, as a good enough mother, I must have the fortitude to stay the course. I may need to go away at times, even at times when I do not want to go away. And yet, I must be willing to bring myself back into the picture later in order that the other might use me again. In Winnicott's terms, the other may try to "destroy" and banish me, but I must be able to "survive" the other's destruction of me. The idea of being "good enough" is related to the fact that I must be able to be around when need be, but I must also be able to be absent when need be.[14]

EDUCATIONAL IMPLICATIONS: THAT TEACHERS MIGHT BE GOOD ENOUGH

Let us now think "immorally" with regard to education. Unfortunately, the use of teachers by students is very much ignored as an educational theme. I suspect this is because modern educational thought is still steeped in a Kantian understanding of moral life. As if to underscore this point, I have had the following experience while I have been writing about this anti-Kantian way of approaching authority: as I have shared this idea of students using teachers with fellow teachers, a response I often get is, "I hope you are not suggesting that students use teachers in an instrumental way." To respond, I prefer to make the following point: "Actually, human beings always operate in ways that are *already* instrumental. There is no way for human beings to become autonomous enough that they might *not* use each other in instrumental ways." That is not to say that students should *harm* teachers by using them. Pragmatic intersubjectivity need not be a slippery slope to harming others. Using others is, simply, how human beings gain agency.

Indeed, ignoring the use of others has been detrimental to educational thought. A dire result of such ignoring has been the advent of Pollyanna-esque narratives of educational progress. Take theories of teaching, for example. They tend to cling to the assumption that there is still a lot of progress to be made so that teachers might better facilitate student learning and student agency. While we try to squeeze the last drops out of our teaching, there is little attention paid to the interhuman mechanisms that allow teaching to be successful in the first place. Student learning and student agency do not happen in schools unless students use other people in ways that facilitate such learning and agency. Pedagogical practices, no matter how much they improve, are of little use if students do not set the stage for their own flourishing through the use of others. Teaching may get better and better, but students will not put teaching to good use unless they are able to use the presence/absence of teachers in ways that enrich students' educational experience.

Educators cling to such silly progress narratives precisely because they do not consider the *use* of teachers by students. When there is no conception of students using teachers, then it follows that educators must carry out whatever progress is to be made. But such user-phobic narratives of progress ignore the fact that teachers are not actually perfectible. Let's face it: there are many teachers who won't ever be *super*. From a Kantian perspective, this seems like a dreadful fact. ("Our children will not all be able to have *the* best teacher, how awful.") In contrast, a *using* perspective suggests that many students will be able to flourish even if their teacher is not *the* best. Indeed, many students *do* flourish even when they do not have the best teachers. Don't we all know of students who have flourished in spite of mediocre teachers? Haven't many students had educational experiences that, while not being at all exemplary, were used by them in agentive ways? Students flourish in many unexpected circumstances. They often flourish precisely because they know how to *use* a given teacher in ways that address their own needs. It may often be the case that teachers need only be good enough, rather than super.

In fact, Winnicott has outlined the intersubjective dynamics that are at stake when a teacher is just "good enough." Drawing on Winnicott's concept of the "good enough mother," we might say that the good enough teacher is one who provides the circumstances for the student to use the teacher's presence (and absence) for her own flourishing. If the student is able to situate herself toward the teacher so that she learns, experiences, and attains agency in ways that would not have been possible without the teacher, then the teacher has acted in a way that is good enough. The "good enough mother" is one who meets, but does not exceed, the needs and demands of her child. Likewise, the good enough teacher is one who meets, but does not exceed, the needs and demands of his or her student.

Importantly, being good enough may have little to do with whether a teacher is perfect, super, or even just good. Being good enough *may* mean being perfect or super, but it may not. Because being a good enough teacher has more to do with the *student's* actions than with the teacher's abilities, it is wrong to say that the progress of pedagogy lies mainly in the hands of teachers. The good enough teacher is one who proves to be enough of a presence so that the student can be sure that she has a person to fall back on if needed, but also enough of an absence so that the student can gain educational agency that is all her own. What is clear about the role of the good enough teacher is that it cannot come to pass without the activity of the student. The good enough teacher, once she has taken on the present/absent role that is required by the student, cannot actually get any better.

In response to this anti-Kantian conception of student agency, one major objection might be raised right away. It might be said that this is nothing but a reformulated argument for educational merit. It might be suggested that pragmatic intersubjectivity is just another way of saying that education is really up to the individual aspirations of students. Is the notion of the "good enough" teacher simply a way of abdicating institutional responsibility for educating students? Does pragmatic intersubjectivity suggest that it is completely up to students to find ways to use teachers in an agentive way? Is this akin to the conservative argument that folks should pull themselves up by their bootstraps?

Not at all. By arguing that current narratives of educational progress are lopsided, I am not arguing that we should give up on making education better, and that it is up to students to flourish for themselves. I am not arguing that there is no more work to be done, but rather that the work that needs to be done should start focusing on the heretofore neglected issue of how students might be encouraged to use teachers. Far from offering a conservative solution, I want to suggest that the only way for progressive education to succeed is for us to take seriously Dewey's pragmatism. Let us take his pragmatism to the intersubjective realm. Educational theory should, at least for a while, stop thinking about what it means for teachers to be great, and start thinking more thoroughly about what teachers can do to set up a "good enough" platform so that students might become empowered to use teachers.

And another objection might be raised. It might be argued that students are already doing too much using, that many students slide through educational experiences, using schools and teachers as a means to get other things in life. Indeed, many students use other people in order to get a grade, get a diploma, and move on with life. This is not the sort of "use" that I am advocating. When students use teachers and schools in this way, there is a denigration of educational experience. In such cases, education is treated as if it is not a part of life, as if it can be *used* to enhance some "real life" that ultimately lies outside of the school. On the contrary, the use of others that I am advocating is one that makes educational experience itself part and parcel of "real life" self-flourishing. And please note, the "get a diploma and move on with life" type of use is already rife in our present Kantian environment. This type of use will hardly be increased simply by introducing the notion of "using teachers" into educational practice. If anything, the type of use that I am advocating may entice students to use education for purposes that are much more immediate than "getting ahead in life," for purposes that are more agentive.

STRATEGIES FOR "USING" AUTHORITY IN EDUCATION

Here, then, are a few strategies to facilitate the use of teachers. First, it is important for educational institutions to stress the notion of student flourishing through the use of others. It is striking that most schools do not advocate such a basic concept. While education has long treated student flourishing as a central aim, there has been remarkably little advocacy for schools as places where students tend to their own empowerment. When student empowerment is advocated, such advocacy is usually focused on the ways that educators might empower students. It is not only educators who need to empower students; empowerment cannot be done all on the teacher's side. Students need to think of teachers and schools as centers of authority, authority they can use to increase their own agency.

Secondly, students must be encouraged to find the right teacher, the one whom they can benefit from greatly. Such a situation is rare in educational institutions as they now exist. Students are not currently encouraged to befriend teachers based on the extent to which those teachers might help them flourish. Such befriending means more than getting the teacher that you really want for a particular class. It means more than listening to other students' opinions of a particular teacher or professor, and then choosing the instructor accordingly. It means that a student might find a teacher who is truly important to him or her, and then continue to go back to that teacher time and time again, whether in a classroom setting or for more informal conversation. In fact, it strikes me that educators really *do* know about this process of "using." However, we do not currently think about it deeply enough, nor do we theorize it in any sustained way. Educators know that those students who flourish as a result of their education are usually the ones who go out of their way to make extra contact with one or more of their instructors. Students should be encouraged to seek out instructors who are "good enough" for their own particular needs wherever they might find them. This may mean that students seek out teachers who are not their "official" teachers, and it may mean that they do so at times that are not "official" class times. The encouragement of students to use instructors should come both at the institutional level and at the classroom level. Students should be introduced early and often to the notion that they can use teachers in schools in order to gain agency, in order to flourish.

Third, there should be venues and times for students to link up with teachers whom they want to use. It is certainly not the case that all students, once introduced to the notion of using teachers, will avail themselves of this practice on their own. The asymmetry in the teacher-student relation is a great barrier to what I am suggesting. Students may avoid such a relation of use out of the hesitancy that comes when one is faced with authority. Therefore, institutional changes must be made that encourage students to use teachers. Certainly, the practice of keeping office hours, and the practice of connecting with students between classes and after school, these practices are already conducive to the use of teachers. Yet, it is presently the case that very few students avail themselves of using teachers during these times. These times are often taken up by more practical concerns such as making up assignments that have been missed, or obtaining clarification about a concept that was not understood during class. The problem with office hours and in-between times is not that they are inappropriate times for students to use teachers, but that these times too easily float from the work of flourishing to the work of classroom catch-up. In order to encourage the use of teachers, it must be well articulated by the educational institution that educational downtimes are times when student flourishing takes precedent over makeup coursework. Students should be encouraged to use these times, and these teachers, for their own purposes rather than for the purposes that have been laid out by the course syllabus.

Fourth, teachers might be oriented toward this perspective of "being used" early on in their training. At least two aspects of "being used" need to be considered, both of which go against the grain of much teacher preparation. To begin with, being willing to be used also means being willing not to be used, paradoxical as this might sound. Teachers must understand that they will never be used by all of their students. Some students will choose to use someone else instead. In these cases, it is imperative that the teacher be willing to let go. From the Kantian perspective of teacherly perfectibility and educational progress, it may be very difficult to accept that I, as a teacher, may not be in a position to empower the very person I would most like to empower. However, from the anti-Kantian perspective of using others, it is quite possible that I, as a teacher, may have a favorite student who simply chooses to flourish with the help of another rather than with my help. As Winnicott notes, human beings cannot use many people at once.[15] Self-flourishing usually depends upon just a few significant others.

Finally, teachers will, themselves, need to be introduced to the concept of being "good enough." A teacher who knows how to help students flourish will know that student flourishing is ultimately something that must be enacted by the student. Once again, this is a paradoxical concept: in order to help a student flourish, the teacher must know that the student *must help herself to the help of the teacher*, and that this is better perfected by the student than by the teacher. Ultimately, this means that a teacher may never need to be "really good." To be "really good" can interfere with whatever the student might do on her own. Instead, the teacher needs to know how to be just "good enough." It may be necessary to warn teachers that being just good enough may not be as fun as being super. As a good enough teacher, one may or may not get recognition for what one does. This is not an easy notion to accept in a profession that prides itself on the meager consolation that student gratitude offers to employees whose wages are embarrassingly low. To be sure, educators and students are most often caught up in a Kantian calculus of autonomous perfectibility. Authority figures need to be used. They need not be perfect.

SELF-FASHIONING IN THE FACE OF AUTHORITY

In my analysis of relational authority, I have so far focused mainly on interpersonal relations, on intersubjectivity. The only nonhuman element of authority that I have so far entered into our discussion has been the educational text. Now I would like to broaden this enquiry by examining one's relation to larger forces of authority, to forces that have influenced students over the course of centuries. If it is true that authority functions as a relation; and if it is true, as I have tried to show so far in this study, that it is possible for students to gain agency within authority relations, doing so through engagement with other people (both present and absent), and with texts—if these things are true, then one would suspect too that it is possible for students to gain agency through relations with other, larger forms of authority. That agency can be attained in these latter cases I take to be true. To this end, I will now attempt to outline in broad strokes what it takes to attain agency in relation to some potent educational forces. Such agency I call "self-fashioning."[16]

Kieran Egan has argued that education has been overwhelmingly susceptible to three major forces, that educators cling steadfastly to three aims: to follow the natural inclinations of the student, to acculturate the student, and to equip the student with a certain foundation of knowledge.[17] Following Egan, we might say that there are three overarching sources of authority in education, sources that are not human, sources that do not dwell in the body of the teacher. Rather, these are sources of authority that are in the educational air, and have been for many centuries. These sources of authority are, to state them concisely: nature, culture, and knowledge. Egan comes up with these three sources of authority by looking at Rousseau's idea that one should be educated according to one's natural inclinations, at the traditionalist idea that education should pass on tried and true cultural goods, and at Plato's academic idea that there are certain pure forms of knowledge to be learned.

In fact, there is a clear-cut philosophical tradition that speaks to our relation to nature, culture, and knowledge. There is a philosophical tradition that aims to deal directly with the various forces of authority at work in this educational triumvirate. It is the tradition of self-fashioning as manifest in the works of two thinkers to whom we have already been introduced: Friedrich Nietzsche, and Michel Foucault. As I will show here, these philosophers of self-fashioning show quite clearly what it means to gain agency in the face of the educational influences of nature, culture, and knowledge. Philosophers of self-fashioning, on whom the remainder of this chapter will focus, deserve our attention because, both in the writing that they dedicate specifically to education and in their other more general philosophical texts, they offer ways that one might negotiate nature, culture, and knowledge in order to enhance the living of one's life. For the philosophical tradition of self-fashioning, life itself is a matter of negotiating these three forces. And, as such a trajectory of thought shows, living one's life fully, to fashion a self, entails negotiating the authority of these life forces. It entails embracing the contradictory forces of culture, nature, and knowledge in order to become who one is. It entails negotiating the paradoxical forces of authority one faces through the becoming of a person, which, in other terms, might be called becoming well-fashioned.

What is interesting to me about these philosophers of self-fashioning, and what I think is important for educational thought, is that they treat these themes at the personal level of the one educated. They ask us to negotiate these contradictory impulses as such impulses arise throughout the course of our lives. By asking us to undergo such negotiations, by showing us how such negotiations are to proceed, these self-fashioners are looking at the primary predicaments of education from the inside out rather from the outside in. For, if it is true, as Egan argues, that educational activity has been hamstrung by clinging to this authoritative triad, it is also true that such educational activity has been clinging to this triad from the outside in. Gazing in at the fishbowl, one can see the whirl of a contradiction. Gazing in at the fishbowl, the conflicting authorities of nature, culture, and knowledge may seem too much to deal with. Yet, there are also times when one must take the perspective of the fish who looks out. Self-fashioners are aquatic philosophers. They are educational thinkers par excellence because they offer advice for the most significant person in education, the one who is to be educated. These aquatic philosophers show us that it is always possible for a student to engage in a relation with authority, no matter how daunting that source of authority might seem.

In the pages that follow, it is my aim to look closely at how Nietzsche and Foucault deal with the contradictory authorities of nature, culture, and knowledge. I will give an in-depth account of the specific ways that Nietzsche and Foucault use these three forces to shape their own lives, and to offer, by extension, a form of self-management that is germane to our own lives. Further, I will point to some concrete ways that self-fashioning might be brought into the practices of those who are being educated.

SELF-FASHIONING: A NIETZSCHEAN PERSPECTIVE

Nietzsche and the Natural

Addressing the theme of self-fashioning, Alexander Nehamas has noted that "Expressions like 'creating' or 'fashioning' a self sound paradoxical. How can one not already have, or be, a self if one is to engage in any activity whatever? How can one not already have, or be, a self if one is even to be conscious of the experiences and views one is supposed to integrate?"[18] Central to any project of self-fashioning is certainly this paradox that Nehamas has noted, namely, that a person who wants to partake in self-fashioning is already in an untenable position. In such a position, one desires to fashion something, a self, yet it is that very self that is already setting the terms for such a fashioning. In such a case, if there is a self to be fashioned, then that self will not be the same self once it has been fashioned. Thus, the self that one becomes will be a different self than the self that one was before. Under such conditions, one is no longer the same self as the one that set the conditions for self-fashioning, and so it is difficult to say whether one can claim that the self is, in fact, what did the fashioning. Under such circumstances, we are left wondering what, if anything, in human life is natural.

Indeed, the project of self-fashioning starts with very different premises about human nature than those premises that are assumed to cause the above paradox. There is a different orientation toward what is natural about the self and what is not. In the work of Friedrich Nietzsche, for example, we find a form of selfhood that actually inverts the above paradox. For Nietzsche, human conceptions of self are based on an overvaluing of selfhood that is particular to the human animal. It is the hubris of the human animal to assume that there is such a thing as a self that one can identify as an unchanging, natural element. The self, Nietzsche reminds us, is "that little changeling."[19] Selves are no more steadfast than any other natural element, no more steadfast than, say, a tree, or a cloud, or a river. The self is not necessarily selfsame from one period of time to the next, no more selfsame than a tree that grows into a different form or a cloud that depletes itself as it rains. What is natural about a self, is, in fact, precisely that it changes, that it is a "little changeling." Selfhood, from a Nietzschean perspective, makes the above paradox uncomplicated rather than paradoxical. Whereas self-fashioning seems paradoxical from the perspective of the natural, steadfast self; from the perspective of the changeling self, such a practice is altogether reasonable.

The problem of the natural in Nietzsche is not solved so easily, though. It is a shallow reading of Nietzsche that posits him as the champion of pure overcoming, as the unfettered self-fashioner. For in Nietzsche, there is also an insistence that there be something steadfast in people. Nietzsche says of "a well-turned out person" that such a person, "has a taste only for what is good for him, his pleasure, his delight cease where the measure of what is good for him is transgressed. . . . He exploits bad accidents to his advantage; what does not kill him makes him stronger. . . . He is always in his own company, whether he associates with books, human beings, or landscapes . . ."[20] In these famous lines, Nietzsche reminds us that the self, even if protean in nature, needs to remain steadfast enough so that one can choose what one values in oneself. If one is to lead a healthy life, then one must be able to discern and cultivate those facets of life that are most healthy. So while it may seem that Nietzsche is at times advocating a view of the self that is completely malleable, it is also the case that he identifies the importance of seeing enough order in one's self to enhance its positive elements while rejecting its negative ones. For Nietzsche, the natural is ever-changing; but, for the purposes of a life well lived, one must interpret out of that change just enough order so that one can "be many things and in many places in order to be able to become one thing—to be able to attain one thing."[21]

Nietzsche on Culture

When Nietzsche refers to being "in his own company," we can also discern his unique stance toward culture. It is in this stance that Nietzsche shows us a brilliant alternative to the two views of culture that are prevalent in today's educational discourses. In current educational thought, culture is usually treated either as a flimsy adjunct to the more serious natural determinants of genetics and psychological hardwiring, or, in the case of social constructivist approaches, it is treated as that which principally influences natural development. Nietzsche's stance, as exemplified in his statement, "He is always in his own company, whether he associates with books, human beings, or landscapes . . ." is quite different from both the essentialist and the constructivist perspectives. How might one, engaged in the project of self-fashioning, think of culture? One might think of it as a self-projection. When one is faced with culture, one is faced not with an impediment to self-formation, nor with the only mode of self-formation available. Rather, one is faced with the various ways that one's self becomes manifest outside the boundaries of the limits of one's body. When one reads, one is to be looking for aspects of self that resonate with the reading. When one is with others, one is to look for the shades of one's fashioning self that inhere in other human beings. Even when one looks at the wonders of nature, one is to look not for what is exterior to the self but for what one can see of oneself in such wonders. Culture is to be used as a mirror held before the self.

Nietzsche's stance toward culture is also addressed in his educational writings. In *Schopenhauer as Educator*, for example, he argues that the benefit of education will never be realized until such a time when education can contribute to the greatness of great individuals.[22] This is precisely to say that the acculturation carried out by educators should be a reverse-mirror acculturation. Education should expose students to the cultural accoutrements that bring out the best of the best in students, that promote the flourishing of the great individual. His model of the great individual was, of course, himself, under the influence of Schopenhauer. It is true that Nietzsche was at this time against the sort of acculturation he saw in democratically oriented education. Education of the masses, he thought, would be an awful leveling-out process for humanity. What is interesting from the point of view of relational authority, though, is *not* Nietzsche's critique of democratic acculturation per se, but rather what such a critique shows us about how Nietzsche conceived of culture in an educational context. For Nietzsche, the acculturation offered by educators need not be construed as an imposition on the "natural." Rather, the culture that education brings to the student should be approached as "a higher concept of culture," a conception wherein culture is that which helps the self become healthy and strong.[23] Such an acculturation will build "the hardest self-love, self-discipline," and self accomplishment.[24]

And what of navigating the natural together with the cultural? Under Nietzsche's description, this navigation takes an interesting turn. For, what turns out to be "natural" about one's self, what turns out to be a deep description of human selfhood, is the fact that the human self is a protean commodity whose steadfastness is merely a psychological necessity to be tolerated as a sort of orienting force. What turns out to be cultural are those elements in the world at large that might be used to benefit the greatness of individuals. As such, there is still a profound difference between the natural and the cultural, but there is not a contradiction per se. Nature is that which must take enough respite from the vicissitudes of the truly random acts of nature so as to have a potential that is identifiable. Culture, in its turn, instead of being at odds with nature, and also instead of *defining* the natural as some versions of constructivist thought might have it, is that which increases the potential of the natural. To navigate the natural and the cultural is to stick with a version of self just long enough to take advantage of the outward circumstances that increase one's human capacity.

The most striking elements of this Nietzschean approach are found in such statements as this: "My formula for greatness in a human being is *amor fati*: that one wants nothing to be other than it is, not in the future, not in the past, not in all eternity."[25] Nature and culture are to be construed not as monolithic entities to which human selves are yoked, but as two possible objects toward which the human being might turn with psychological intensity. *Amor fati*, love of fate, has a characteristically Nietzschean ambivalence toward the natural and the cultural worlds. One is left wondering whether what is advocated is a love of one's natural lot, or whether it is a love of one's cultural allotment. And then as if to make the distinction between the natural and the cultural even less important, there is the added psychological nuance that human beings should hone in themselves the capacity to *embrace* these objects as one embraces any other object of affection. Nature and culture, whichever of them is actually being referred to, are light matters, matters that we might embrace or cast off at our choosing. To navigate well, we should embrace both. The same ambivalent lightness is evident in the inside-out teleology of Nietzsche's injunction, "Become who you are," and in the introjected causality of his claim, "Thus I willed it."[26] In such statements Nietzsche urges us to navigate the natural and the cultural, and he suggests how: we must embrace such injunctions and such claims whenever possible.

Nietzsche on Knowledge

As for knowledge, Nietzsche's position is most easily summarized by the following health warning: knowledge can be dangerous to one's health. Just look at Nietzsche's critique of knowledge acquisition and his championing of forgetfulness. With regard to acquisition, Nietzsche reminds us that it can often happen, in fact does often happen, that the more one pursues knowledge, the less one has a chance to cultivate the self in healthy ways. Commenting on scholars, and by extension all those who spend much of their lives in the pursuit of knowledge, Nietzsche notes the following: "We are unknown to ourselves, we men of knowledge—and with reason. We have never sought ourselves."[27] Here we are reminded, in a somewhat lighthearted way, of the absent-minded professor, or of Socrates who was known to lose himself in thought for hours at a stretch. But Nietzsche is quite serious about this matter. He has studied the *psychology* of epistemology and notices that human beings tend to lose touch with themselves when they dedicate themselves to learning.

> "The objective man," writes Nietzsche, "is indeed a mirror: he is accustomed to submit before whatever wants to be known, without any other pleasure than that found in knowing and 'mirroring'; he waits until something comes, and then spreads himself out tenderly lest light footsteps and the quick passage of spiritlike beings should be lost on his plane skin."[28]

When one becomes focused on knowledge, one can become a human mirror, unable to look selfward. At least that is the health risk of knowledge acquisition. We people of knowledge "are necessarily strangers to ourselves, we do not comprehend ourselves . . . we are not 'men of knowledge' with respect to ourselves."[29] Nietzsche's words here are self-explanatory.

To complement this critique of knowledge acquisition, Nietzsche offers a self-fashioning strategy—the strategy of forgetting. On the flip side of learning, there is forgetting, forgetting that has been historically denigrated as a sort of epistemological lack, forgetting which Nietzsche instead champions as a necessary antidote to the experience of being turned into a human mirror. One can recuperate one's self-focusing strength, and one can get rid of unhealthy, knowledge-focusing habits. This has been done in the past by people who are willing to practice forgetfulness. Nietzsche remarks that it "is the sign of strong, full natures in whom there is an excess of the power to form, to mold, to recuperate and to forget."[30] He reminds us of the French author "Mirabeau, who had no memory for insults and vile actions done him and was unable to forgive simply because he—forgot."[31] To forget, rather than being a sign of weakness, is, for self-fashioners, a positive way to deal with the agglomeration of knowledge that tends to turn us away from our selves.

AN EDUCATIONAL STRATEGY OF SELF-FASHIONING

Faced With the Authority of Nature

At this point, I should make it more clear how such a philosophy of self-fashioning, concerned as it is with authorities natural, cultural, and epistemological, is important for educational practices. It seems to me that education *writ large* has a certain reticence to think about these themes even though these themes are so inescapably involved in teaching and learning. For example, with regard to human "nature," I would submit that, as we go through educational experiences, we, as learners, need ways to think about what we might do with our "natural" capacities. I would submit, along with Nietzsche, that one cannot get away from making judgments about what one is good at learning, what one does well, what one likes to learn, as well as what one is not good at, what one does not do well, what one does not like to learn. We are, to go back to Nehamas's point, beginning in all educational instances with a self, and it would be very difficult *not* to make certain judgments about that self. When learning to speak a foreign language, for example, does one not right away make judgments about whether one is good at speaking that foreign language? And even once that initial judgment is made, do we not make further judgments about what particular aspects of learning that foreign language we are good at? Are we not constantly making judgments such as, "I am very good at conjugating verbs, but not so good at memorizing vocabulary?" To make a judgment such as "I am good at conjugating verbs," or "I am not good at conjugating verbs" is precisely to make a statement about what one's *natural* capacities are.

My point here is not to show the various ways that one identifies something natural in one's capacities as a learner, but rather to say how important it is to take such an act of identification as a specific theme in education. When it comes to what seems natural and what does not so seem, one should have an educational strategy. Such a strategy should entail at least two steps. The first is the simple identification of what one does well and what one does not. This first step is already too common.[32] But the second step is one that is so well illustrated by philosophies of self-fashioning: one should have a stance and a mode of conduct vis-a-vis the natural. Yes, judgments about what comes naturally are all but unavoidable in education. However, it is possible that such judgments can themselves be used as an educational tool to increase one's human capacity. When I discover that I *naturally* enjoy reading poetry more than I enjoy reading novels, that is only a preliminary judgment on the natural. Questions that follow are the more important questions such as, "What do I make of this enjoyment?" "Is this an enjoyment that I want to cultivate?" "Is this an enjoyment that I want to inhibit?" "Is this enjoyment one that is tied to other enjoyments that I might bundle together in order to enrich how I live my life?" Secondary questions such as these do not just assess the natural. They make the natural an integral part of how one fashions one's self.

By taking the "natural" self as something to be fashioned, one willingly ignores, or one chooses to forget, to borrow Nietzsche's idea, disciplinary practices that hinder one's flourishing. Instead, one makes of one's life an artwork. One treats matters of self as if they are matters of shaping, fashioning, embellishing, and elaborating. This treatment is in direct opposition to procedures that would identify, quantify, and "treat" the human being. In fact, the difference between the two senses of the English word *treat*, serves to underscore the difference between self-fashioning and just plain living one's life. When one lives a modern life, one tends to become enmeshed in disciplinary systems. One is diagnosed and often "treated" by juridico-medico discourses. Yet self-fashioning offers another way to "treat" oneself. One stands back from oneself and treats oneself as a painter would treat her painting. One chooses what formulas to apply to the self, and what formulas to shed. In the disciplinary treatment, one is subjected to steadfast remedy. In the self-fashioning treatment, one partakes in self-molding.[33]

Faced With the Authority of Culture

A strategy with respect to culture is similarly important for educational flourishing. Just as one might identify a natural inclination, one will certainly be able to identify educational agendas that stem from cultural imperatives. And these cultural imperatives may not be in sync with what one enjoys to do, or with what one can easily do. A strategy of self-fashioning, however, will serve to highlight, and build upon, the cultural-ness of these cultural imperatives. In other words, a person with a self-fashioning orientation will recognize that the cultural has a form that must be juxtaposed with the natural. In the case of acculturation, too, there should also be a two-part strategy.

The first part would consist of the student identifying those aspects of education that are thoroughly cultural, those aspects that clearly go against the grain of one's natural inclinations, those aspects that seem to be public interventions rather than private blossomings. However, this first step in self-fashioning would be initiated by the student rather than the educator. The first step in self-fashioning would entail identifying aspects of acculturation that truly rub one the wrong way. Are there not always requirements in education that one simply does not agree with, that are said to be necessary because one will not "fit" in society without so conforming? Perhaps the matter at hand is as simple as the quality of one's handwriting. Perhaps it is a more central aspect of one's identity such as forced gender conformity. Perhaps one has a reaction against being a responsible citizen. A first step would be to make such identifying part and parcel of the student's educational experience.

Once again, this first step is not enough. It is not enough for one to identify such cultural norms. Educational rhetoric aimed at "producing thoughtful consumers," "developing responsible citizens," and "training students to succeed in the workplace"—such rhetoric has long identified acculturating ends. Educators have long taught students the requirements of culture. And certainly, students have long identified those aspects of acculturation against which they then choose to rebel. A second step to self-fashioning would entail moving beyond the Manichean binary of acceptance or rebellion. A second step would entail taking an active stance toward things cultural. While it may be that most of us have had a reaction to acculturating imperatives, and while it may be that some of us have resisted such imperatives over the course of our educational experience, how many of us have pushed forward with the myriad ways one might conduct oneself toward the cultural? Such questions as these might be asked about the cultural imperatives toward which one has an aversion: "Is this a cultural imperative that needs to be resisted? Would such resistance behoove me?" "If I do resist, do I want to resist in ways that avoid confrontation, or would it behoove me to *create* confrontation?" "Are there other cultural imperatives that are more important for me to resist than this one?" "Which resistances will be most healthy for me?"

At this point, the following objection might be made: Doesn't this sort of stance serve to depoliticize people? When we speak of what is most healthy "for me," does it not undercut the more admirable aim of educational acculturation? The aim of creating democratic citizens? To answer this objection, I turn to the work of Michel Foucault on self-fashioning.

Foucault points out that, actually, the goal of self-fashioning is as much about one's political orientation as it is about what might seem, at first blush, to be a matter of individualism. In educational interactions today, one is often hard-pressed to encourage serious political engagement on the part of students. Such failure may rest on a failure to understand the profound ways in which the political bears on practices of self. For the philosophers of self-fashioning, the self is the starting place for the ways one orients oneself toward freedom. Thus, practices of self are about the self per se, but they are also about the ways in which one orients oneself. One cannot orient oneself toward the political when the self is disregarded. Current thinking on the distance of the self from the political is the remnant of humanist, Cartesian thought that takes the self to be a thinking machine that thinks on other objects rather than on itself. This is what Foucault means by remarking that "there are more secrets, more possible freedoms, and more inventions in our future than we can imagine in humanism as it is dogmatically represented on every side of the political rainbow."[34] The political, as Foucault has shown in his genealogical works, serves to discipline and punish people at the level of self. Thus, for one to orient oneself toward freedom, one must work at the level of self at the same time that one works at the level of structural and cultural change.

Faced With the Authority of Knowledge

And toward knowledge, a self-fashioning education will also entail a strategy. The first step is to identify some of the ways that knowledge gets used in one's life. Let us take the example of a student who enjoys reading poetry. Questions such as these might be raised: What does my knowledge of poetry do for me as I live my life? How much of my life is spent reading poetry? Has poetry increased the quality of my life? Or, are there ways in which poetry has detracted from the quality of my life? Are there certain periods of my life when poetry has been more useful, certain periods where it has been less useful? These first-step questions are actually not at all common in modern thought, which tends to look at knowledge as benign. Philosophers of self-fashioning, and in particular Nietzsche, take a radical stance toward knowledge. Their stance is one that questions the very usefulness of knowledge if such knowledge does not increase the capacity of human beings. Following a self-fashioning strategy, one will not assume that learning poetry is necessarily beneficial. Knowledge of poetry, for example, is only beneficial to the extent to which it gets put to good use in one's life. Learning itself is not good use. Good use comes when learning enhances one's life.

A second self-fashioning relation toward knowledge might include the meta-understanding that knowledge can be as dangerous as it is beneficial. Certainly such an understanding flies in the face of modernist epistemologies. And, it flies in the face of current conceptions of education, especially ones that uphold knowledge accumulation as the litmus test of a successful education. Modern epistemologies, as inaugurated by Descartes' privileging of thinking over feeling, tend to have a the-more-knowledge-the-better orientation. This is all too evident in the push toward ever-increasing student achievement. If there is one attitude that philosophers of self-fashioning certainly have in common, it is the warning that knowledge is not innocuous.[35] Indeed, when it comes to knowledge, one who self-fashions may be willing to put reins on the mind. And this stance toward the mind will be different from the popular mantra that we should enhance thinking skills rather than learn content. As a self-fashioner, even thinking skills may be dangerous if they are not in sync with what one needs to increase one's human capacity. To flourish as one who self-fashions, all things knowledge-based might be let go if need be.

Certainly, this sort of letting-go takes a great amount of courage. It takes courage to let go of one thought and pursue another. Michel Foucault has spoken about the courage to self-fashion one's thinking as follows:

> As to those for whom to work hard, to begin and begin again, to attempt and be mistaken, to go back and rework everything from top to bottom, and still find reason to hesitate from one step to the next—as to those in short, for whom to work in the midst of uncertainly and apprehension is tantamount to failure, all I can say is that clearly we are not from the same planet.[36]

These words were written at a time when Foucault was under attack for the change of course in his thinking. Some have claimed that he went back on his previous thinking when, in his later writings, he turned to self-fashioning. Yet, those who make such a claim have precisely failed to see the courage of thought that is entailed when one turns one's back on previous thought, when one takes one's self in a new direction.[37] Educational institutions are the sorts of places where the courage to think in new directions should be fostered. Self-fashioning will certainly entail courage of thought.

A third step is to self-fashion using the specific techniques with which education equips us. One such technique is fluency in writing. Philosophers of self-fashioning such as Nietzsche and Foucault, and as well others such as Socrates and Michel de Montaigne, have shown us that writing can well be used as a technique of self. With regard to writing, Foucault has noted the following:

> The main interest in life and work is to become someone else that you were not in the beginning. If you know when you

began a book what you would say at the end, do you think
that you would have the courage to write it?[38]

When he makes these sorts of statements, we are reminded that
the tool of literacy is a great aid to the project of self-fashioning. Such
a stance toward literacy is much different than a stance that advocates
"finding one's voice" through writing. Within a writerly pedagogy of
self-fashioning, one will become other than what one is in part through
the interchange that takes place between who one is to begin with and
who one's writing makes one become. This self-fashioning perspective
on writing is especially important given current educational strategies
vis-à-vis literacy. It is striking that while schools do tend to encourage
students to practice all the trappings of the writing profession—encouraging creativity, proper documentation, precise conceptual thought, etc.—
they tend not to encourage the very trait that makes literacy so very
important to those who are truly engaged with writing as a form of life.
Writing is a means to self-modulation. Writing can be, in the context of
an education oriented toward self-fashioning, a means to become who
one was not before.

DEEP IMPLICATIONS OF RELATIONAL AUTHORITY

Self-fashioning thus orients one toward the natural, the cultural, and
the epistemological.[39] Yet my point is not that one should first *identify*
the natural, the cultural, and the epistemological aspects of one's educational experience, and then make the best of one's education in light
of these findings. It is not that at all. For, the natural, the cultural, and
the epistemological can too easily be identified and taken as steadfast
attributes of one's educational experience. To identify such aspects only
is precisely to *stop* self-fashioning. My point is rather that one's stance
toward nature, culture, and knowledge needs to be *educated* all along
the way. In fact, I cannot imagine—at least not after having read such
self-fashioning thinkers as Nietzsche and Foucault—any reason to ever
assume that the matters of what should be one's stance toward nature,
culture, and knowledge could ever be ascertained once and for all. It is
precisely the brilliance of philosophers of self-fashioning that they show
how these fundamental educational concerns are actually lifelong problems. One's life cannot be identified first, and then practiced later. That
is the mistake made by one who lives one's life in a stilted way. Similarly,
one cannot be educated first, and then proceed to live one's life after
education has ended. Both self-fashioning and education proceed through
modulation. Self-fashioning and education proceed through an ongoing
engagement with the authority of nature, culture, and knowledge.

If this chapter has shown anything, it is that treating authority as a relation has deep consequences. To understand authority as a relation, we must rethink Kantian morality. We must rethink the popular educational focus on pragmatism. We must be willing to "use" other people. We must rethink how we orient ourselves toward larger bodies of authority. We must rethink how we choose to remember, and how we choose to forget. We must rethink how we understand the personal and the political. We must even rethink the self, itself. That is, we must rethink dearly held notions about self-integrity. We must wonder if self-constancy is so important after all. What I am trying to say here is that relational authority is not just about authority. It is also not just about relation. It is about a paradigm shift that requires serious changes in a Western belief system that has long used *non*relational authority as a fulcrum point for understanding human beings. To be sure, this chapter has only sent out feelers. It has only begun to intimate the myriad, deep, philosophical implications that follow once we embrace the relationality of authority. These sorts of deep implications deserve better treatment than I can give in this short book. For, the present study is not meant to be an extended treatise on modern philosophical trends, but is rather oriented toward authority in educational settings. With this aim in mind, the next chapter will address an educational matter whose boundaries are better defined. It will address the relation of authority when educators pose questions.

CHAPTER 5

Questioning Authority

I have always called myself a progressive educator. Thirteen years teaching in junior high and high schools. Eight years of university teaching. I have called myself a progressive educator in part because I have always liked the progressive orientation toward authority. As we have seen earlier in this book, the progressive position comes with definite assumptions about the nature of authority, about how authority is *not* a thing to be trusted. I have liked this progressive discomfort with authority. Along with embracing progressive pedagogy, I suppose I have embraced a few other progressive commonplaces. For example, over these twenty-one years, I have usually been sure, as I believe many progressive educators have been sure, that lecturing to my students is an unnecessary imposition of authority. I have been sure that asking students questions, and eliciting their answers, is less imposing than straightforward teacher-talk. I have understood questioning as a fair and just way for students to interact with authority, while I have understood lecturing as an un-needed showing-off of the teacher's knowledge. I have preferred the former. At least that *used to be* the case.

My confidence in questioning was shaken some time ago when I had a conversation with a friend of mine who was trained to be a lawyer at Harvard Law School many years ago. When I told her about the way I favored questioning over lecturing, her response was unqualified: "While there might be some merit to questioning, let me tell you . . . Socratic questioning, of the law school variety, is the most authoritarian form of education I have ever experienced. As law school students, we used to be cowered into submission. Law professors frightened us to death with their knowledge of the law, and with our own

111

lack of knowledge. They did this all without *telling* us anything. It was all by questioning."

These remarks have certainly made me think. They have challenged one of the commonplace assumptions that I have been making for many years now. These remarks have reminded me that I, too, used to make some fairly *non*relational assumptions about authority. Let me explain. When I have, in the past, favored questioning over teacher-talk, I have been making the assumption that some forms of authority are more relational than others. I have been assuming that questioning is a more dynamic way for students to interact with the authority of the teacher, while lecturing is a static way for teachers to impose their authority. Yet now I notice something that I used to miss about the practice of questioning. It is this: if all authority is relational, then the distinction I used to make—the distinction between the authority of questioning being dynamic and the authority of a lecture being static—simply does not make sense. Authority is dynamic, period. Thus, if there is any benefit to educational questioning, it must come from the questioning interchange itself rather than from the fact that questioning is a "more relational" way of enacting authority. My friend's remarks, together with the relational conception of authority that I am offering in this book, suggest that the matter of educational questioning cannot be solved so easily. We must not be pre-satisfied, simply because it has become a progressive commonplace, that questioning is somehow impeccably beneficial in education.

In this chapter, I look into the authority that gets enacted through the question-answer exchange between teacher and student. Since this entire book is focused on the relation of educational authority, it is very important that we look at educational questioning. Why? Quite simply because if commonplace assumptions about authority map, in various ways, onto various teaching techniques, then such assumptions map onto the practice of educational questioning in the most direct way possible. Since the aim of this work is to challenge commonplace assumptions about authority, then there is no more practical way to go about it than investigating the relation of educational questioning. Today, various educational camps such as the three that I have mentioned before—the progressive, the traditionalist, and the critical—make commonplace assumptions about questioning. These assumptions derive from their respective stances toward authority. My aim is to break through the progressive commonplace that questioning students forms the basis of a kinder and gentler pedagogy. I also want to break through the traditional commonplace that lecturing is altogether unharmful. And I want to break through the critical commonplace that lecturing is unharmful as long as it aims toward social justice.

QUESTIONS AND THEIR HIDDEN STATEMENTS

This chapter's investigation of questioning will rely on the work of Hans-Georg Gadamer. Gadamer's work affirms, as I have mentioned above, that an investigation into the authority of questioning is highly instructive. Indeed, Gadamer goes so far as to say that "[t]o understand meaning, is to understand it as the answer to a question."[1] So he sees in questioning a wide range of ramifications including meaning itself. Gadamer's analysis helps us to understand that questions are more intimately connected to statements than we might think. In terms of education, it might seem easy to claim differences between a pedagogy of questions and other sorts of pedagogies, such as ones that mainly tell. It might indeed seem that a pedagogy that questions exercises less authority than a pedagogy that does not question. As a literature teacher, for example, one might tend to be confident that the use of a question, one that asks, "What do you think about such and such a passage?"—that such a question enacts less authority than the use of a statement that tells students, "This passage means such and such." However, as we shall see, Gadamer's analysis of the question shows that these sorts of assumptions need to be reconsidered.

Gadamer notes that the structure of the question puts finitude into play in the same way that the thought of one's own mortality puts the finitude of existence into play. Writes Gadamer,

> It is clear that the structure of the question is implicit in all experience. . . . From a logical point of view, the openness essential to experience is precisely the openness of being either this or that. It has the structure of a question. And just as the dialectical negativity of experience culminates in the idea of being perfectly experienced—i.e., being aware of our finitude and limitedness—so also the logical form of the question and the negativity that is part of it culminate in a radical negativity: the knowledge of not knowing.[2]

In the same way that notions of human finitude and death suggest the limits of what can be experienced, the use of a question intended toward an object presents us with the possibility that such an object may not exist as we originally thought. As Gadamer puts it, the question "breaks open the being of the object."[3] "The significance of questioning consists in revealing the questionability of what is questioned."[4] "The sense of every question is realized in passing through this state of indeterminacy, in which it becomes an open question."[5] In this way, the question presents us with mortality. It presents us with the possibility that existence, in the form of whatever object is subject to the question, is not as we heretofore thought. It presents us with the possibility of the death of the object as we know it. A question, in contrast to a statement, is posed in order to emphasize the possibility that an object may be otherwise. While a statement explains the living attributes of an object, a question presents us with the possibility that the object may not exist at all. While a statement confirms, a question disconfirms.

Another aspect of the question is that it actually contains a statement within. In a sense, it might be said that the statement is only a subset of the question. Let me explain this in Gadamerian terms. For Gadamer, the question is that which orients us toward a field of possible experiences. The question provides a framework for the sort of experience that a group of interlocutors will be in a position to think about. It provides us with what might be called a "spectrum of experience." In this way, a question is not simply a reminder that an object of questioning may cease to exist as we know it; it is not just a statement about the *limits* of experience. A question opens up possibility at the same time that it suggests the limits of possibility. As Gadamer puts it, "A question places what is questioned in a particular perspective."[6] A question situates, and it opens up an inroad with regard to the object.

Thus, the spectrum of experience begun by the question implies both a limit and a field of possibilities. The question suggests the limits of its answers at the same time that it asks for possible responses. A "Why?" question demands a "Because" response. A "Who" question demands that a person be named. "Posing a question," notes Gadamer, "implies openness but also limitation."[7] A question establishes the range of possible experiences that may come into play within the process of questioning and answering. When the question is answered, the spectrum of possible answers will be bound by the question. To put Gadamer's point succinctly, we might say that *every question contains the seed of its own answer*. A question implies its own statement.

THE "TRUE QUESTION"

And while it might seem that the question, described in the above way, overdetermines its own answer, Gadamer is quick to point out that it is possible to pose questions in such a way that the answer will not be overdetermined. He writes of the difficult, but possible, practice of asking what he calls a "true question." It is possible to question in such a way that the question itself, while sowing the seeds of its own answer, drives right for that spot where the answer is truly unknown to both the questioner and the respondent. In such a case, the questioner will ask about something she really does not understand:

> To ask a [true] question means to bring into the open. The
> openness of what is in question consists in the fact that the
> answer is not settled. It must still be undetermined, awaiting
> a decisive answer. The significance of questioning consists in
> revealing the questionability of what is questioned.[8]

So for Gadamer, the hermeneutic, horizon-posing structure of the
question does not preclude the questioner from creating space where
she honestly searches for information from the other. While the questioner has a definite horizon from which she asks the question, there is
still space within that horizon to query about that which is not yet
known. As Gadamer says, "Discourse that is intended to reveal something requires that that thing be broken open by the question."[9] So,
while my own understanding may limit the subject of my questioning
to the objects that are within my cultural and historical purview, I will
still be able to identify some objects within that purview as objects that
I do not fully understand. I can cause an object, one that I only catch
a glimpse of from my present horizon, to be "broken open." I can catch
myself up short. I can identify objects that, while available to my understanding, are not fully understood without the help of an other.
When I can cause an object to be "broken open," only then have I
posed a "true question" about that object.

BUT CAN A TEACHER ASK A "TRUE QUESTION"?

What we must ask, though, is whether a *teacher* can ask such a true
question. According to Gadamer, the act of posing a "true question"
falls apart when it comes to teachers who actually have curricular aims.
Teachers *do* have something in mind that they want their students to
learn. We *do* want our students to know how to factor an algebraic
equation. We *do* want our students to know that John Dewey was an
American Pragmatist. We *do* want our students to be able to place
Langston Hughes within the historical context of the Harlem Renais-
sance. While it may be possible for the ordinary person engaged in
dialogue to ask "true" questions, questions that intend to *really* question, to break the object of question open, to truly put that object into
question; while it may be possible for the ordinary person, from
Gadamer's perspective it appears that the ordinary *teacher* is actually
hamstrung by her commitment to conveying a certain body of knowledge. A teacher, as opposed to just any old someone, must choose
questions with possible answers in mind. That is to say, it would be a
very strange pedagogical situation if a teacher were to question her
students without a preconceived notion of which answer she hopes to

elicit from them. Teachers, after all, enact authority. A law school professor, as opposed to any old questioner, can be frightening because she knows exactly where her questions are to lead.

Another way to say this is that the pedagogical pressure to elicit *specific* answers from students, as opposed to any old answer, is the difference between general dialectic and pedagogy. It is certainly possible to imagine a teacher asking completely open-ended questions: "What did you think of the first chapter of Toni Morrison's *Sula*?" "What is your interpretation of John Dewey's notion of "experience" in his book *Experience and Education*?" "What do you think the answer to $2X + 8 = 0$ is?" However, it ceases to be pedagogy and becomes general dialectic if the teacher does not intervene to steer answers in a direction that she favors.

With this sort of logic Gadamer surmises that it is not actually possible for a pedagogical question to be "true." Talking about the true question, Gadamer notes that there is a paradoxical difficulty with any true question that would be posed by a teacher. The paradox inheres in the fact that the teacher himself would have to disappear. As Gadamer puts it,

> Every true question requires an openness. Without it, it is basically no more than an apparent question. We are familiar with this from the example of the pedagogical question, whose paradoxical difficulty consists in the fact that it is a question without a questioner.[10]

That is to say, as soon as a teacher must ask a "true question," then she ceases to exist *as teacher*. So for Gadamer, the teacher can only pose false questions. If she poses true ones, then she ceases to exist. This is Gadamer's Cartesian motto of the questioning teacher: "I pose false questions; therefore, I exist."

TEACHERS CAN ASK TRUE QUESTIONS

But we should say more about "true questions" than Gadamer does. Gadamer intimates that teachers cannot pose true questions. Is he correct? I would say not. It is precisely at such a juncture that we should stop listening to Gadamer even while taking his notion of the "true question" to heart. In other words, we should heed his philosophical insight, but disregard his educational perspective. Gadamer moves in a very subject-centered direction with regard to the "true question." First, he describes the nature of a true question, its nature being that it cracks open the object. This description we should cling to. This description is very consistent with the "linguistic turn" of poststructuralist thought, the turn that gives ontological priority to the linguisticality of human experience. While language, in general, is constitutive of human experience, the question, in particular, is deconstitutive of the subject matter to which it refers.

However, when Gadamer claims that some folks can ask true questions while some cannot, he slips into the subject-centered assumption that language is ultimately a tool under the employ of human intentions. At this point he forgets the important lesson of his instructor, Heidegger, that language is the house of Being, rather than Being being the house of language.[11] When Gadamer claims that the pedagogical question presents us with a "paradoxical situation," we must note that Gadamer is making a subject-centered correlative to the linguistic structure of the question. At this point, he is indicating that some people will be less "true" in their questioning by virtue of what they *intend*. While it may be a fact that a teacher cannot have scot-free intentions, it is not a fact that these tainted intentions will automatically derail the deconstitutive nature of a question. A teacher can indeed "break open" an object. This is because a teacher's intentions do not completely determine the outcome of dialogue. In Gadamer's analysis, the notion of the "true question" becomes confused with the more subject-centered notion of *asking a question in a true way*. Can there be an educational scenario in which subject matter can be broken open? The answer is, "Yes." Teaching intentions will never be pure, it is true, but that does not mean that pedagogical questions will not break open the subject matter at hand. Teachers *can* pose true questions.

To make it clear how true questions can be posed, it is helpful to draw on Gadamer's own conception of language, and then to borrow a metaphor from Gilles Deleuze. As Gadamer's conception of language reminds us (perhaps as a reminder that his "paradox of the pedagogical question" is not such a paradox), language does not result from the intentions of individual speakers. Instead, language is enacted in the in-between space of dialogue with an other. Language is the practical consequence of intersubjective engagement, rather than the transition of messages from one interlocutor to another. As Gadamer himself writes, "[L]anguage is by nature the language of conversation; it fully realizes itself only in the process of coming to an understanding."[12] That is to say, language becomes what it truly is by way of its enactment within the to-and-fro of dialogue. Likewise, a question is only a question within the context of the interlocutors' engagement with that question. Thus, when a question is posed, it is on the field of human interaction where its "truth" is worked out. Whether a question is a "true question" will depend upon the subject matter that it "breaks open" during conversation. To say that a teacher's question is automatically "false" even before the dialogue has begun is to ignore the intersubjective life of language. It is to confuse the intention of speech with the communal enactment of conversation. A teacher *can* pose a true question because such a question is always poised to be enacted relationally, between teacher and student. Such a question is always poised to be worked out somewhere down the line, sometime after the question has been posed.

There is, of course, one more problem to be worked out with regard to the "true question" posed by a teacher. Given that a true question poses its own field of possibilities; given that a true question breaks open its subject matter; given that a teacher does have certain intentions; and, given that questioning gets worked out in the in-between of human dialogue—what, then, might "true" questioning look like in education? While the specificities of each interchange will vary, I want to offer the following Deleuzian metaphor.[13] A question, truly enacted, will be much like the rolling of dice. When a pair of dice is rolled, the field of possible outcomes is bounded, to be sure. Only combinations of one through six will result. At the same time, though, the object under consideration, the resulting combination, cannot be manipulated by the dice roller. Combinations will be "broken open" each time the dice are rolled. Of course, it cannot be said that the dice roller lacks intentionality. She wants the dice to roll, without doubt. My point here is that we can take the dice roller in this case to be the teacher who questions.

The main difference between questioning, on the one hand, and throwing dice, on the other, is the importance of keeping subject matter in play. Picture a pair of dice that is thrown into a wobbling box. These questioning dice, unlike others that might be thrown onto a stationary table, will be thrown by the teacher into a wobbling box that is held on one side by that teacher, and on the other side by the student. It is the interaction of teacher and student that must keep the question (the dice) in play for as long as the subject matter at hand requires a questioning attitude. Such a gaming process suspends the intentionality inherent in the philosophy of the subject, and it inaugurates an intentionality that does not want to know exactly what its own outcome will be. It signals a break from the sender/receiver model of language, and it requests an openness toward subject matter that searches for answers that are not necessarily known beforehand. Within the questioning process, the aim of communicants is not *erklären*, but rather *verstehen*. The aim of questioning is not to *explain*, but rather to *understand*.

A teacher *can* ask a true question in spite of Gadamer's claim that he or she can't do so. Gadamer's insight is that there is teacher authority being enacted in questioning scenarios. Unfortunately, he jumps to the conclusion that such authority keeps the teacher from being able to ask true questions. His insight is that the teacher's questions cannot have a pedagogical purpose without exercising the authority to steer answers in this direction or that. His mistake is to say that such authority spoils the essence of the question. With his insight we should agree; with the mistake we should not. The questioning process in education exercises authority as a sort of ontological prerequisite—this is the insight of Gadamer's that we should explore.

Let us approach this insight by first summarizing what we have learned about the difference between questioning and telling. While it is tempting, following progressivist sensibilities, to jump to the conclusion that questioning is a process that exercises less authority than telling, the situation now seems quite different. Telling relies on an exercise of authority—that is certainly true. Indeed, when a teacher tells his students, "This passage means such and such," or, "The answer to this problem is X = –4"—by such statements, a teacher is enacting authority to the extent that the student must accept these statements as true. However, as far as the exercise of authority goes, telling is not in fact different from questioning. While telling relies on an exercise of authority that guarantees the veracity of a teacher's statements, questioning also relies on an exercise of authority. Like telling, questioning would not have any grounds on which to proceed if it were not based on authoritative enactment. In this way, we cannot say that there is an appreciable difference between the authority of telling and the authority of questioning. Both pedagogical telling and pedagogical questioning enact authority as a prerequisite for *being pedagogical*. Without such an enactment of authority, educational telling would not effectively convince, and educational questioning would not properly steer.

But having said all this, I am not trying to say that we should settle into complacent equanimity. It is now tempting to claim that questioning is no more, and no less, overbearing than telling. It is tempting to say that it really does not matter whether we tell our students what they need to know, or whether we question them about curricular matters. After all, the question involves the same sort of authoritative steering that the statement does. Indeed, I would agree to this sort of equanimity to some extent. I think it is correct to say that when it comes to questioning and telling, neither one is inherently more imbalanced than the other. Questioning, per se, is not *more* innocuous than telling. But once we have said that questioning and telling in education are both enactments of authority, it is important to go farther. We must ask if questioning might be more dominating at some times than at others. When might questioning be, as my lawyer friend has said, "the most authoritarian form of education I have ever experienced"? When might it be less authoritarian? To address this matter, I turn, as I have a number of times in this book, to an analysis of language itself.

THE AUTHORITY OF QUESTIONING:
ITS SIGNIFIER AND SIGNIFIED

The linguistic distinction between the signifier and the signified sheds some light on instances when a question might be more authoritarian, and when it might be less so. A question is certainly different from other forms of speech. It is different from a statement. In a statement, there is a certain authoritative link between speaker and phrase. For example, if I, as a teacher, *state* "this passage from Ernst Gaines's novel means such and such," it is clear that the person who ensures such a statement to be true is I, the instructor. When I say that "this passage means such and such," I am the one who is obligated to stand behind what I say. In such a case, I am enacting authority. The statement is true to the extent that one trusts my authority as a teacher. It is true to the extent that a student enters into the authority relation that has been inaugurated by my statement. To put this in linguistic terms, the teacher, by virtue of being authorized, *signifies* some aspect of the world. When I am a teacher, my statement *signifies* the truth about Gaines's novel, and it does so by virtue of authority. In this sense, the instructor's statement takes the role of signifier while the truth about Gaines's novel is what is signified. What motivates the signifier/signified connection? By this I mean, why does my statement signify some truth, just as the word *chair* might signify some real chair? The instructor's statement signifies the signified because there is an enactment of authority. Authority is the glue that cements signifier and signified. It makes the pedagogical statement believable.

Compare this to *questioning*. When a teacher questions, it seems, at first blush, that the teacher gives over the signifier/signified pair to the student. When I, as teacher, ask a student, "What does this passage from Ernst Gaines's novel mean?" it seems that the question places the student in a position to signify the meaning of the passage. It seems as if the student's answer will now stand in relation to the truth of Gaines's text as the signifier does to the signified.

However, the difference between the signifier/signified pair of a teacher's statement, on the one hand, and the signifier/signified pair of a student's answer to a question, on the other, is that the latter pair does not exercise authority in the same way. When the student answers a question, there is no "glue" of authority. Instead, the teacher remains the one who applies the glue by means of steering the dialectic. As Gadamer has shown us, pedagogical questions are *pedagogical* precisely because they are enacted through authority. One does not "give over" authority by changing the way one talks, by changing from statement to question. One does not make glue available to the student, as it might seem at first glance. Instead of being a "giving over" of authority, questioning is a ventriloquizing of authority. The question makes authority seem to be on the side of the student, while in fact, the glue remains on the side of the teacher.

Questioning does not really give over the signifier/signified pair (together with its glue) to the student. The questioner retains a new, glued, signifier/signified pair even as he conceals that retention. When I ask about a certain passage, it is true that my words no longer signify the passage's meaning. It is true that my question no longer signifies some fact that I want my student to accept. However, questioning simply *personalizes* the signifier/signified pair. *Now my words signify the meaning of the question in my head. I am the text being interpreted by my question. My question signifies the meaning of me.* And in this new signifier/signified relation, it is still the teacher who is being authorized. As in the case of the statement, authority still shores up a certain signifier/signified relation. Because I enact authority in the process of asking the question, my question holds together. My question is now glued to *me.*

I find this signifier/signified relation between the teacher and her question to be very important. For, this relation goes a long way toward distinguishing between the forms of questioning that are more dominating and those that are less dominating. The question will be more dominating when the authority enacted during questioning is not readily visible to the student. When teachers act as if authority is being "given over" by posing a question, then they are hiding the authoritative workings of the question. This leads to domination. The authority of the question itself, the authority enacted as the teacher's words signify her own meaning—this authority should not be hidden from view. Questions dominate to the extent that one ventriloquizes without admitting that there is ventriloquism going on.

The problem with Socratic method that dominates does not rest solely in the fact that such a method uses forceful questions. It lies rather in the fact that the questioner stands in such a relation to the student that the authority of questioning is not open to critique. When the gluing of authority is elided from view, then questioning leads to domination. On the other hand, if the student is in a position to *question the question*, then such questioning is less dominating. Questioning will be less dominating when the student is able to recognize that there is no *natural* link between the signifier and signified, that there is no *natural* reason that the teacher should get to signify her own meaning. Questioning will be less dominating when the student is able to realize, instead, that there is "steering" lodged even in questions that seem innocuous, that there is authority being enacted even in questions. It will be less dominating when teacher and student wobble the box. The question itself must be on shaky ground.

NON-SUPERFICIALITY, HUMILITY, CIRCUITRY

So one way for a question to be less dominating is for the authority of the question to be exposed. How else can the question work in healthy ways? To answer this means proceeding with our hermeneutic inquiry. Three themes that such an inquiry offers I will call: non-superficiality, pedagogical humility, and circuitry.

By non-superficiality, I mean the hermeneutic insight that linguistic interaction, interaction such as questioning, is not simply a topical way to address the more serious matter of content. Questioning need not be conceived as just one way, among many, that a particular content can be broached. From the perspective of philosophical hermeneutics, the linguistic practice of questioning is instead intimately linked to the content at hand. That is to say, there is not a hierarchical relationship between language and being, between what we say and what our saying represents, between pedagogy and curriculum content. Instead, language and being are human states that are ontologically equal. Questioning and content are on the same ontological plane.

Gadamer explains this relation of language practices to human experience with this succinct statement in *Truth and Method*: "Being that can be understood is language."[14] That is to say, linguistic formations are not in a representational relation to human experience. A word does not signify a thing. Instead, a word, a phrase, and in the case that interests us here, a question, are all intrinsic to the being-understood of the thing. Linguistic forms are synonymous with the ways that human beings come to understand the things of this world. Following Gadamer, there would be no human understanding without the linguistic forms in which humans participate. And more specifically, there would be no questioning sorts of understandings if there were no questioning statements. "The coming into language of meaning," writes Gadamer, "points to a universal ontological structure, namely to the basic nature of everything toward which understanding can be directed."[15] In other words, linguistic forms are a necessary phase in the process of human understanding. Language is not a tool that is used to understand subject matter. Rather, language enacts subject matter. Language brings into being the understanding of subject matter. Or to let Gadamer state this point as he has put it in his interchange with Habermas around the scope of hermeneutics, "[T]here is no societal reality, with all its concrete forces, that does not bring itself to representation in a consciousness that is linguistically articulated. Reality does not happen 'behind the back' of language . . . reality happens precisely *within* language."[16]

Thus, the authority of the question is not superficial. A question is not a supplement to content in the sense that it is an annex, an addition enabling students to understand the more serious matter of content. Rather, questioning is a particular linguistic form that insinuates itself into the very content that is being understood. Questioning is a "supplement" to content in the more invasive sense that I have outlined in the fist chapter. A question becomes part and parcel of the content at the same time that it supplements. In this way, questioning cannot be said to be simply one mode, among others, by which curriculum is presented. It cannot be said that the question is a mere matter of presentation. For, questioning, as linguistic practice, is integral to that which is questioned. Questioning enacts the authority of content. It becomes part of the content, authorizing content into life.

In this sense, a question that empowers will be "non-superficial." When a question is posed, it should not be posed as a technique or as a method. It should rather be posed in the true spirit of exploration. Content can be authorized into life by the question, if the question is treated as it should be treated: as part of the emergence of content itself. A question that empowers will not be a test. It will not aim to expose what the student does not know. It will not even aim to show what the student *does* know. Its aim will be understanding itself. A question must not be treated as a mere adjunct to the more serious matter of learning content. To be empowering, a question will go to the depths of the subject matter under consideration. An empowering question will thus create new understandings. It will not serve as a teaching technique. It will not solidify understandings that the teacher already has in mind.

Another property of the question, one highlighted not only by hermeneutics but by Platonic dialogues as well, is the question's ability to encourage pedagogical humility on the part of the instructor. It is in the nature of the question to authorize such humility. Gadamer speaks to the humility that can be fostered by the question when he reminds us, in *Truth and Method*, of Socrates:

> Among the greatest insights that Plato's account of Socrates affords us is that, contrary to the general opinion, it is more difficult to ask questions than to answer them. . . . In order to be able to ask, one must want to know, and that means knowing that one does not know.[17]

Questioning, as we have seen, is different from stating to the extent that there must be some desire to break open the object in question. And in this desire to break open the object, there will necessarily be an admission that one does not know all about the object. To ask a question, one must *want* to know, and we should take this locution of wanting in both its senses. First, asking a question means that we *desire* to know. But also, asking a question means that we *lack* knowing something. To ask a question in this way is an admission of incompleteness. It is in this way that questioning enacts an authority that questions its own authority. A question throws its own authority into question.

Gadamer reminds us of the comic thematics of Platonic dialogues when Socrates' interlocutors mistakenly think that asking questions is easier than answering them: "When the partners in the Socratic dialogue are unable to answer Socrates' awkward questions and try to turn the table by assuming what they suppose is the preferable role of the questioner, they come to grief."[18] Questioning must not be considered a cavalier act, an act that can be carried out without thought or deference. While it may be easy to ask a question of another person when the aim of the question is to reaffirm self-knowledge, such a question, as we have seen, is no more a question than it is a statement. The matter of serious questioning, questioning that intends to break open the object, requires deference with regard to the object. Haven't we all had the experience, as teachers, where we find ourselves slipping into an *easy* mode of questioning, a mode where we ask a question whose answer we want parroted back according to what we already have in mind? In such a circumstance, isn't there a sense in which we feel that our question is not a question after all, but is actually a statement in disguise? As Gadamer notes, "To someone who engages in dialogue only to prove himself right and not to gain insight, asking questions will indeed seem easier than answering them."[19] Questioning that does not aim to subsume otherness in the name of the same is not easy. It entails the labor of identifying one's own ignorance.

The "true" question, then, gets enacted through a practice of deference. It is striking how such deference gets overlooked even in progressive pedagogies that claim to be student-centered. For instance, while there is much focus on the experience of the child in the work of Dewey, it is ironic that there is not mention of the existential humility that must accompany any serious inquiry that intends to put subject matter into question. One would think that being child-centered has the existential correlate of being teacher-decentered, but such is not necessarily the case in progressive pedagogy. For example, when Dewey stresses, in *The Child and the Curriculum*, how the teacher must "psychologize" the link between student and subject matter, there is no sense that humility is central to how educators approach their relation to student and subject matter. In fact, the opposite is more the case. Following Dewey, it is assumed that the teacher must know *more and more* in order to facilitate learning on the part of the child.[20] Indeed, the very group of educators whom we suppose we might look to for humility vis-à-vis the student lets us down. And the same is true in the more obvious cases of educators who hail from traditional and critical backgrounds. Rather than advocating humility, there is a tendency among progressives, traditionalists, and criticalists alike to stress the ways in which teachers need to know *even more*, that such a surplus of knowledge needs to be applied with great confidence by teachers if they are to educate students in today's rapidly changing world. But an analysis of the question reminds us that confidence and surplus are not altogether happy matters in the realm of education. And importantly, one can be authorized, by means of questioning, to affirm the significance of that which is *not* known.

Another aspect that questioning brings to the fore is the way authority *circuits* between self and other. By this I mean that a "true" question cannot actually be asked without beginning a circuit in which the original question is responded to by *another question* on the part of the student. As Gadamer reminds us, questioning puts the student and teacher into the mode of a circuit, a mode wherein each is the asker of questions. It is not simply that the teacher asks questions and the student responds. Rather, any response that is a genuine attempt on the part of the student to let the question speak to him or her, such a response will itself be a question. Thus, questions are not unidirectional. They run back and forth between teacher and student. A detailed hermeneutic explanation of this circuitry is in order since such back-and-forthness goes against commonsense understandings of questioning and responding.

Whereas a rough-and-ready sketch of questioning would, unproblematically, show the teacher questioning and the student answering, Gadamer maintains that such a question/answer exchange is not what actually happens when a teacher and a student are addressing questions in earnest. Actually, the question will be answered *by a question*. To see this, first recall how Gadamer understands the nature of questioning. Questioning is characterized primarily by the process of self-critique, or humility. It is enacted through the process of suspending one's own judgments in order to truly question some object, to admit the aspects of an object that one doesn't know. But as Gadamer reminds us, this process of suspending judgment is precisely what occurs also in the case *where one is the recipient of a question!* To be open to a question, one must also suspend one's particular point of view in order to make meaning out of the question that is posed. Thus, within the process of responding to a question, the structure of posing that same question also comes into play.

Gadamer explains this process as follows:

> Understanding begins ... when something addresses us. This
> is the first condition of hermeneutics. We now know what this
> requires, namely the fundamental suspension of our own preju-
> dices. But all suspension of judgments and hence, a fortiori, of
> prejudices, has the logical structure of the question.[21]

In order for a question to be understood by the one to whom it is
posed, it is not enough for the question to be posed. In addition, the
person toward whom the question is intentioned must be open to the
question's meaning. That is to say, the one questioned must be just as
open to an exploration of the object in question as the questioner is
himself. To return to our metaphor of the wobbling dice box, the one
questioned must be involved in keeping the dice in play. Such openness
requires a "suspension of judgments and hence, a fortiori, of prejudices" that will allow space for the object to be scrutinized by the one
questioned. In order to entertain a question, one must put in check all
hasty judgments, all overdetermined understandings, about the object in
question. In short, one must undergo the same self-critique that the
questioner undergoes. "The essence of the question," notes Gadamer,
"is to open up possibilities and keep them open."[22] One must, in this
fundamental sense of acquiring a questioner's humility, *become* a questioner in order to understand a question.

To be more clear, let us work through this circuit from teacher to
student, and back again: To ask a question, the teacher must let her
guard down and admit that the object in question is not entirely understood. So when the teacher asks a question, she is approaching an
object in a particular way, in a way that emphasizes the extent to which
that object is unknown from her perspective. This is the only way a
teacher can approximate a "true" question, namely, from a stance of
humility that admits there are certain ways in which the object is unknown to her. But as Gadamer reminds us, the teacher's self-critique
applies not only to the teacher but to the student as well. Given that the
question is intended toward the student, the particular situatedness of
the teacher's self-critique has implications for the student's understanding of the question. The question gets its meaning from its particular
vantage point, its particular humility, the particular way in which it
"breaks open" the object. And, this particular self-critique cannot be
lost on the student without the question losing its meaning.

Gadamer explains the circuitry of the questioning process as follows: "To understand a question means to ask it. To understand meaning is to understand it as the answer to a question."[23] In other words,

the process of questioning, once begun by a person in a particular situation, requires that the recipient of the question must walk in the shoes of the questioner, must experience the questioner's particular situation. The one questioned must do more than simply acquire a questioner's humility. She must also acquire the particular humility that the questioner used to pose the question in the first place. The one questioned needs to be able to think through the question from the questioner's position, or, in other words, she must be in a position to pose the same question in the same way. This is to say nothing of answering the question. We need not know whether the one questioned is yet in a position to answer. The point here is that even to get to an understanding of the questioner's question, the one questioned must, herself, be in a position to pose a question (to roll the dice) that gets at the same questionableness that was proposed in the first place. The circuit of questioning, from the teacher to the student, creates a circuit in which questions always follow questions.

But let us once again take a step beyond Gadamer. Whereas Gadamer focuses on the circuitry of the question, it is possible to glean a significant insight about authority from this notion that the question reduplicates itself within the response of the one questioned. It is possible to consider the authority of pedagogical questions in a different light, namely, as an authority that authorizes further questions. The circuitry of questioning will prompt the teacher to listen closely to the student's response. In this way, after the initial question has been posed, the teacher is prompted to turn around and become the student of her own student. She is prompted to see the student response as an authoritative source. The teacher, by virtue of treating the student's response as a question (rather than treating it as an answer that is simply insightful or not, simply correct or incorrect), is prompted to search for the ways that the student's new question might lead to further learning. She is prompted to see her own question as the beginning of a circuit that begs for more questions. The authority of the question authorizes not only the meaning of content and the humility of the questioner. It also authorizes the questioning circuit to continue.

QUESTIONING AND THE AUTHORITY RELATION

In elementary school classrooms, in middle schools, in high schools, in universities, during music lessons and dance instruction, when parents teach their children, and at almost any time when education is taking place, questioning sooner or later comes into play. As I have tried to show in this chapter, questioning has ramifications for the authority relation, but not in the way that some people, including myself, have assumed. Questioning does not simply make the authority relation more gentle, nor does is simply intensify the authority relation. Instead, questioning has a circuitry of its own that may bear one way *or the other* on the authority relation. As I have shown, the circuitry of the question needs to be considered in light of hermeneutics, in light of language theory, and in light of the attitudes questioners and answerers adopt toward the object they are questioning. And as I have also shown, questioning in education cannot be distinguished so easily from other forms of interaction. Questioning is not so different from making statements as one might think.

Certainly, this last matter, the complicated relation between statements and questions, has implications for educators who claim that a pedagogy of questions is less authoritarian than a pedagogy of statements. One such educator is Paulo Freire, who will be the focus of the next chapter. In his work, *Pedagogy of the Oppressed*, Freire condemns the practice of narration in education, and praises instead his problem-posing method of pedagogy. As he says, much oppressive education is suffering from "narration sickness."[24] Oppressive educators narrate too much, and ask questions too little. After the work that has been done in this chapter examining the nuances of similarities and differences that exist between the authority of questions and statements, I do not think that Paulo Freire is remiss in coming to the initial conclusion that the authority of questioning is fundamentally different than the authority of narrating. I think his work simply needs to be augmented. Freire's work on problem-posing education goes part of the way toward explaining the relational life of authority. But, his work needs to be augmented with a theory of authority-in-relation, a theory of the sort that I have been proposing throughout this book. The final chapter will address this matter, in addition to offering some concluding remarks.

CHAPTER 6

Paulo Freire and Relational Authority

In his famous text on education, *Pedagogy of the Oppressed*, Paulo Freire makes a claim about authority that is very bold, yet seemingly uncomplicated. Freire claims that through *his* type of education there will no longer be any problems with authority. His type of education is a problem-posing form of pedagogy, one that aims to liberate students and teachers from the ideological and physical domination practiced by rulers and elites. In the problem-posing pedagogy of liberation that Freire describes, "arguments based on 'authority' are no longer valid." Instead, authority will "be *on the side of* freedom."[1] While this claim about authority is presented as uncomplicated, I would like to suggest that such a claim can only be made if we first delve into the *relations* involved in Freirean pedagogy. Further, I suggest that the relations involved in Freirean pedagogy are relations of the psyche. To understand authority in Paulo Freire, we must understand relation therein. To understand relation in Paulo Freire, we must understand relation as a psychic phenomenon.

In this chapter, I argue that Freirean education needs a psychoanalytic theory to deal with the relation of authority.[2] And by extension, I mean that any pedagogy which aims to enact authority in ways that enhance the capacity of students and teachers needs to take the psyche into account. Without recourse to psychoanalytic thought, Freire's work falls into a nonrelational, and more thoroughly liberal, understanding of authority. With a full-fledged use of psychoanalysis, though, Freire's thought establishes a way of understanding educational authority that

129

no longer falls into the either/or binary of authority on one side, and freedom on the other. Authority *can* advance the cause of freedom. It can do so if we understand authority as a psychic relation. It can do so if the authority relation does not succumb to the unwanted psychic extremes of domination and submission.

BANKING AUTHORITY WITHOUT THE PSYCHE

To begin with, though, I want to leave the psyche out of our conversation in order to highlight what Freire's treatment of authority is like *without* any reference to the unconscious. Such an approach I find useful in order to highlight certain gaps that exist when such an omission is made. This means describing "banking education," which is Freire's trope for educational authority, without referring to issues of psychic domination and submission. Without such referents, banking authority ends up being much like other liberal notions of authority. Theories of liberalism assume that authority is detrimental. Liberalism tends to refute *all* authority, with no room for compromise or nuance, because the elimination of authority is seen as the only avenue for attaining freedom. In such a schema, banking authority falls on the oppressive side of the dichotomous split between authority and freedom.

At the risk of repeating what is common knowledge, a restatement of Freire's banking model helps to show what kind of authority is at work therein. The banking model is remarkable for at least five oppressive operations. Each of these operations is enforced by the authority of the banking instructor. First, banking authority uses methods that force students into the passive position of an active/passive dichotomy. Some examples of this active/passive dichotomy are: "the teacher teaches and the students are taught," "the teacher knows everything and the students know nothing," "the teacher thinks and the students are thought about," and "the teacher disciplines and the students are disciplined."[3] In this binary of what-the-teacher-does and what-the-student-does, the teacher is always the initiator of pedagogical practice and the student is always the one for whom such practice is initiated. The banking instructor is an authority figure who takes the active position of oppressor. The student is in the passive position of the one who is oppressed.

Second, banking authority uses *epistemological* force to strip the learner of human agency. Describing the banking system, Freire shows the convergence of epistemological and existential agency. To know for oneself is also to *be* for oneself. And conversely, to have another person think in one's stead is to lack the ontological position of being completely human. When banking authority is used on a person, that "person is not a conscious being (*corpo consciente*); he or she is rather the possessor of *a* consciousness: an empty 'mind' passively open to the reception of deposits of reality from the world outside."[4] Fullness and emptiness are first of all descriptions of *knowledge* that has been acquired or not. At the same time, though, they are descriptions of the extent to which human *existence* is fully, or only partially, actualized. Banking authority forces epistemological passivity onto students, which is in fact no different from forcing them into existential passivity.

Third, banking authority is used to dominate the other by separating pedagogy into two parts. Splitting curriculum in an artificial manner, the preparation of content is done by the teacher only. The student does not witness that preparation, and thus the banker keeps the student out of the loop of human agency. Writes Freire,

> The banking concept (with its tendency to dichotomize everything) distinguishes two stages in the action of the educator. During the first, he cognizes a cognizable object while he prepares his lessons in his study or his laboratory; during the second, he expounds to his students about that object. The students are not called upon to know, but to memorize the contents narrated by the teacher.[5]

What the banking teacher does in his or her preparation of knowledge ensures that the student's relation to curriculum will not be an agentive one that *engages* with knowledge, but will rather be a passive one that *looks at* predigested knowledge. Students are force fed what Charles Schwab has called a "rhetoric of conclusions."

Banking authority also works as an ideological apparatus. Freire notes that "[b]anking education (for obvious reasons) attempts, by mythicizing reality, to conceal certain facts which explain the way human beings exist in the world."[6] Such education promotes commonsense understandings of the world that are not to be questioned. These are the "myths" to which Freire is referring. In a banking system, people do not "develop their power to perceive critically *the way they exist* in the world *with which* and *in which* they find themselves."[7] Instead, they see their world "as a static reality."[8] So banking authority creates static myths about the world. And, it also creates static myths about language. The very words that come to be used by teachers and students are shrouded in the common sense of dominant ideology. Within the banking system, students are not able to interrogate language. They cannot say "a true word."[9]

Moreover, banking authority sets up house inside of the student's consciousness, instilling its own slogans and its own policies *within* the student's worldview. Drawing on Hegel's Master/Slave dialectic, Freire describes this situation as the same as the consciousness of the slave who internalizes his or her master's values. Banking educators fill the oppressed "with slogans which create even more fear of freedom."[10] The oppressed, " 'housing' the oppressors within themselves . . . cannot be truly human."[11] This is because the oppressed are " 'beings for another.' "[12] "What characterizes the oppressed is their subordination to the consciousness of the master," and this subordination is augmented by the practice of banking authority, a practice that is quite happy to let students experience the world vicariously, as an inauthentic part of the student self.[13] After being banked, students can no longer think for themselves because their thinking is only borrowed from an other. Likewise, they can no longer *be* for themselves because their very being is borrowed from that other.

In short, banking authority uses various means to oppress the student. The banking system employs authority at the expense of the student's freedom. Such authority produces passive students, denies epistemological/existential agency, severs the student from knowledge production, fosters dominant ideologies, and introjects itself into student consciousness. As Freire points out, "The teacher confuses the authority of knowledge with his or her own professional authority, which she and he sets in opposition to the freedom of the students."[14] Authority, in the banking system, is antithetical to freedom.

HOW TO STOP BANKING?

A Familiar Refrain

Freire's analysis is convincing, and it forces a pressing question: How can educators combat this banking authority? I would like to begin answering this question by referring to a familiar refrain, one that I hear almost every time I expose my own students to this text by Freire. This refrain might seem familiar to those who remember reading Freire for the first time, or to those who have asked their students to read *Pedagogy of the Oppressed* in the classroom. The refrain is, "Stop banking." Indeed, this is one way to read Freire, namely, that his text is primarily a warning against the banking system. Along with this refrain, I usually get the message that what Freire wants teachers to do is give up authority in the classroom. To use the banking system, it is reasoned, means being authoritarian in the classroom. In order to give up the banking system, and to empower our students accordingly, authority must be yielded.

This refrain has a long history in the liberal tradition, echoed at least since Kant's *What is Enlightenment?* The refrain is that authority is always the enemy of freedom. As John Dewey points out in "Authority and Social Change," liberal notions that pit authority *against* freedom derive from the Enlightenment attempt to escape two very specific forms of authority: the Church and the State.[15] Yet, what started out as the rebellion of individuals against these specific censuring institutions became generalized into a "demarcation of two separate spheres, one of authority and one of freedom."[16] Dewey describes this process:

> The final result was a social and political philosophy which questioned the validity of authority in *any* form that was not the product of, and that was not sanctioned by, the conscious wants, efforts, and satisfactions of individuals in their private capacity—a philosophy which took the form of *laissez faire* in economics and all other social and political affairs. This philosophy claimed for itself the comprehensive title of liberalism.[17]

Authority and freedom are one of those binaries against which Dewey is always railing, and it is a binary that can, at first glance, seem to be what Paulo Freire is trying to underscore with his denunciation of the banking system.

But the results of such a liberal abdication of authority do not necessarily succeed, at least not in escaping the banking situations that Freire describes. Giving up authority, on the part of the instructor, does not necessarily lead to agency on the part of the student. It simply leads to less authority on the part of the instructor. When one stops exercising epistemological force, that does not *necessarily* lead to the other's existential agency. That the instructor is no longer the sole arbiter of ways of knowing does not guarantee that the student will become empowered as a knowledge seeker. Nor does showing students the preparation of content guarantee that the student will herself come any closer to the construction of knowledge. Giving up authority also does not guarantee that dominant ideology won't continue to trump progressive notions. And, abdicating authority may decrease the internalization of alienating positions; but, there is no guarantee that students will rid themselves of internalized otherness that has already taken place. In general, we can't know how an abdication of authority will empower students; we can only know that there has been a withdrawal. Liberalist assumptions about the withdrawal of authority are based on the false logic that if A works to the detriment of B, then not A will automatically foster the capacity of B.

Dialogics Against Banking

Freire's own answer to the problem of authority is, of course, the application of a dialogic, problem-posing pedagogy. For Freire, a dialogic approach helps dissolve the dehumanizing effects of banking authority, encouraging instead humanization. The dialogic approach is supposed to work against banking authority on all of the levels that I have outlined above. For the purposes of this analysis, though, I will focus on the most significant level, namely, the imbalance created by banking authority: the imbalance that pits teacher against student in a relation of one who is active (the teacher) versus one who is passive (the student). As Freire argues, this is the fundamental opposition that needs to be resolved: "[T]he practice of problem-posing education entails at the outset that the teacher-student contradiction to [sic] be resolved. Dialogic relations—indispensable to the capacity of cognitive actors to cooperate in perceiving the same cognizable object—are otherwise impossible."[18] Dialogic education is supposed to end the passive/active teacher-student dichotomy that characterizes banking pedagogy.[19] While the banking system activates teachers and pacifies students, the dialogic model will rectify this relationship. The teacher-student relationship will be subject to revision. Instead of teacher and student, there will be teacher/student and student/teacher.

Linking together the matters of dialogue, activity/passivity, and teacher authority, Freire writes:

> Through dialogue, the teacher-of-the-students and the students-of-the-teacher cease to exist and a new term emerges: teacher-student with students-teachers. The teacher is no longer merely the-one-who-teaches, but one who is himself taught in dialogue with the students, who in turn while being taught also teach. They become jointly responsible for a process in which all grow. In this process, arguments based on "authority" are no longer valid; in order to function, authority must be *on the side of* freedom, not *against* it.[20]

Notable in this passage, first of all, is that Freire is trying to get away from the liberal paradigm of authority, where authority is pitted against freedom. This is clearly implied in the claim that authority will be "*on the side of* freedom, not *against* it" in the dialogic approach. Yet also notable in this passage is Freire's own inability to actually get out of liberalism's authority versus freedom dilemma.

There are two ways that Freire fails to escape this dilemma. The first is that he fails to give up the very terms that are at stake. Freire's claim that "arguments based on authority are no longer valid" is still very much an argument based on authority. While Freire offers a different configuration of those terms, he does not get out of the general param- eters that are already establish by the liberal conversation about author- ity.[21] While Freire troubles the authority/freedom binary by putting authority on the side of freedom, he does not give up the binary itself. He refutes the mutually exclusive nature of authority and freedom, but does not provide any nuance for understanding the difference between the two. It is at this point that Freire falls into what Michel Foucault has called "the trap of the Enlightenment."[22] By accepting the terms of the Enlightenment (in this case the authority-freedom dichotomy), one finds oneself in a position where it is not possible to escape the Enlightenment gambit without seeming to advocate an irrational position.

A second problem with Freire's solution to the freedom and au- thority dilemma is that he reconciles the pair simply by fiat—*let there be* authority on the side of freedom. But putting authority on the side of freedom does not ensure that authority will not continue to be op- pressive. There have been many historical cases where a movement's authority, or the authority of an enlightened leader, continues to be oppressive in the very name of freedom. Freire knows this is a problem. He struggles with this concern in *Pedagogy of the Oppressed* when he wonders if someone could practice a banking education in the name of the oppressed. His conclusion is that it is *not* possible to liberate and to bank at the same time:

> In the revolutionary process, the leaders cannot utilize the banking method as an interim measure, justified on the grounds of expediency, with the intention of *later* behaving in a genuinely revolutionary fashion. They must be revolu- tionary—that is to say, dialogical—from the outset.[23]

But in response to this admonition against using the banking method even for expediency's sake, we must ask of Freire: What is the difference between "authority *on the side of freedom*" and "the banking method as an interim measure"? Within the discussion that has been established in *Pedagogy of the Oppressed* on the banking system as an authority- driven pedagogy, there is no substantive difference. Authority on the side of freedom is the same as the use of the banking method on the side of freedom. By putting authority on the side of freedom by fiat, the very notion of authority becomes hollowed out to the point where it is meaningless. Freire does not solve the authority/freedom dilemma be- cause does not offer a substantive account of what authority actually does once it is on the side of freedom.

Now, it is clear to me that Freire does not mean to say that the banking method should be on the side of freedom. What happens to Freire's account of authority is that it gets stuck in a nonrelational way of thinking. To say that authority will be on this side or that is to ignore the relational dynamics of authority. It is to remain under the spell of liberalism. It is to stop short of true dialogic thinking. Freire's pedagogy is relational. It is dialogical. Unfortunately, he does not push his relational thinking all the way through to the matter of authority. Authority will never be on the side of freedom because, as we have seen, authority is not some "thing" that takes sides. Let us rather say, *"The authority relation will foster freedom"*—such a statement is relational. Such a statement honors Freire's dialogic project. To give meaning to such a revised statement, we must take the psyche into account. In the above paragraphs, I have intentionally ignored Freire's allusions to psychoanalysis. The psychic life of problem-posing education is not fully developed in *Pedagogy of the Oppressed*. But it should be. Without it, Freire's account of authority stops short of being relational. To push Freire's relational thinking all the way through to the matter of authority, it is necessary to push farther with his psychoanalytic leanings.

PSYCHOANALYSIS IN PAULO FREIRE: FROM AUTHORITY TO BALANCE

When the metaphorics of *Pedagogy of the Oppressed* are scrutinized, it becomes apparent that there are too many allusions to psychoanalytic thought to ignore. Terms such as "domination," "submission," "unconsciously," "guilt," "alienation," " 'neurotically,' " "sadism," "masochism," "internalization," and "necrophilia" are used in ways that evoke psychoanalytic sensibilities. Moreover, Freire's text makes explicit use of the psychoanalytically inspired work of Eric Fromm, Herbert Marcuse, and Franz Fanon. Freire's seminal text is indeed indebted to psychoanalysis in many ways. Attention to Freire's psychoanalytic references yields a much more subtle understanding of the place of authority in dialogic education. Such attention yields a notion of authority that does not succumb to the "trap" of the Enlightenment. Attention to Freire's psychoanalytic stance points to a conception of *pedagogical authority as balance* that is Freire's unique contribution to the problem of authority vis-à-vis freedom in education.

Authority is explicitly considered from a psychoanalytic perspective in *Pedagogy of the Oppressed* as Freire relates Erich Fromm's psychoanalytic work on child rearing to the matter of domination in education. Paraphrasing Fromm, Freire comments on authoritarianism in the family:

> If children reared in an atmosphere of lovelessness and op-
> pression, children whose potency has been frustrated, do not
> manage during their youth to take the path of authentic
> rebellion, they will either drift into total indifference, alien-
> ated from reality the authorities and the myths the latter
> have used to "shape" them; or they may engage in forms of
> destructive action.[24]

At stake here is the submission, of the child, a submission that is facilitated by the authority of a parent who dominates, using his or her
authority in a destructive way. Freire's point here is that banking authority reenacts the authoritarian ways of households.

Authoritarian instructors also force students into submission, into
a state of being dominated by the other. Freire goes on to describe the
teacher's role as one-who-dominates. Teachers, even if they mean well,
are too often caught in a psychic equation that is difficult to get out of
because the equation started long ago during their own submission as
children. Writes Freire,

> Well-intentioned professionals (those who use "invasion" not
> as deliberate ideology but as the expression of their own
> upbringing) eventually discover that certain of their educa-
> tional failures must be ascribed, not to the intrinsic inferior-
> ity of the "simple men of the people," but to the violence of
> their own act of invasion. Those who make this discovery
> face a difficult alternative: they feel the need to renounce
> invasion, but patterns of domination are so entrenched within
> them that this renunciation would become a threat to their
> own identities. To renounce invasion would mean ending
> their dual status as dominated and dominators.[25]

The authority figure in the unhealthy banking system, like the parental
authority in an imbalanced family system, practices domination. Authoritarian instructors are caught replaying circuits of domination and
submission with their students.

FLESHING OUT THE CIRCUIT
OF DOMINATION AND SUBMISSION

To further unpack the relation between authority and domination/sub-
mission, it is helpful to look again at Jessica Benjamin's rendition of
psychoanalysis. Benjamin describes domination and submission in a
manner that glosses the intricacies of parental and teacher authority to

which Freire alludes. Her analysis, like Freire's, is based on an analysis of dialogic interaction between self and other. Also like Freire's, it is based on the sort of struggle for recognition that is described in Hegel's dialectic of recognition between master and slave.

As you will recall, Benjamin offers an account of the self as involved with the other in a struggle for recognition that may be balanced and healthy, or that may denigrate into a relationship of domination and submission. Self and other may find balance in their recognitive relations, or they may become stuck at the poles of oppressor and oppressed. What I will argue here, with the help of Benjamin, is that Paulo Freire's solution to the problem of authority finds its resolution in a psychoanalytic notion of *balance* between the poles of domination and submission.[26]

Recall that Benjamin describes an interaction between self and other that is grounded in the double life of self. For Benjamin, human encounter between self and other is best understood in terms of the intersection between the domain of fantasy and the domain of reality. Balance, domination, and submission all happen on the fault line between these two domains. One domain, it will be recalled, is that of fantasy. She terms this domain "intrapsychic" space. It is

> the inner world of fantasy, wish, anxiety, and defense; of bodily symbols and images whose connection defy the ordinary rules of logic and language. In the inner world, the subject incorporates and expels, identifies with and repudiates the other, not as a real being, but as a mental object.[27]

The bonds formed in intrapsychic space are based on my ego's needs and drives. They are based on my own way of understanding the world. These bonds are rigid. They congeal in the psyche if they are not tested by experiences that are not in my own psychic control.

This description of intrapsychic space resonates with Freire's own description of the objectification that happens in banking interaction. As Freire notes, "banking education begins with a false understanding of men and women as objects."[28] Such objectification happens, writes Freire borrowing the words of Eric Fromm, in the space of fantasy as the banking educator

> is driven by the desire to transform the organic into the inorganic, to approach life mechanically, as if all living persons were things. . . . Memory, rather than experience; having rather than being, is what counts. The necrophilous person [the banker] can relate to an object—a flower or person—

only if he possesses it; hence a threat to his possession is a
threat to himself; if he loses possession he loses contact with
the world. . . . He loves control, and in the act of controlling
kills life.[29]

The oppressor is one who objectifies the other. Such objectification
takes place as one controls the image of the other, holding the other in
the private space of fantasy, subjecting the other to one's own control,
killing the subjective life of the other.

Distinct from the objectifying bonds formed in intrapsychic space
are those formed in intersubjective space. These bonds are exterior to
the self. These bonds are experienced during fleshly encounters with the
other. As Benjamin explains, intersubjectivity "refers to that zone of
experience in which the other is not merely the object of the ego's need/
drive or cognition/perception but has a separate and equivalent center
of self."[30] An intersubjective bond is established when I interact with an
other who is *not* under my control, who is radically separate from me.
Whereas the intrapsychic bond involves internal, psychic manipulation
of the other, manipulation that turns the other into an *object* of fantasy,
the intersubjective bond involves recognition of the other as a subject
with agency.

This distinction—between the intrapsychic and the intersubjective—
is in fact akin to a similar distinction upon which Freire relies: Martin
Buber's distinction between the I-It and the I-Thou. Freire calls upon
Buber, noting that "the antidialogical, dominating *I* transforms the
dominated, the conquered *thou* into a mere *it*."[31] In such a relationship,
the self refuses to be with the other in an intersubjective way. In contrast to this *I* that treats the other as an *it*, Freire recommends "the
dialogical *I*." He points out that such an dialogical *I*

> knows precisely the *thou* ("not-*I*") which has called forth his
> or her own existence. He also knows that the *thou* which calls
> forth his own existence in turn constitutes an *I* which has in
> his *I* its *thou*. The *I* and the *thou* thus become, in the dialectic
> of these relationships, two *thous* which become two *I's*.[32]

A Thou, which Buber calls a "center of surprise," must be an other who
is unexpected and thus thoroughly out of the control of the I who
acknowledges this Thou.[33] It is this surprising, intersubjective Thou to
which Freire links his dialogic pedagogy.

Following this distinction that both Benjamin and Freire make
between the domain of fantasy and that of reality, we find that domination occurs when either of these two domains take over completely.

It is dangerous for self and other to live in a world that is primarily fantasy and objectifying, but it is likewise dangerous for self and other to live in a world that is full of too much unexpectedness, too much Thou-ness. Domination and submission follow from either extreme.

For example, when I interact with an other, domination can result if I continually cast the other in forms that are lodged in the psyche, in ways that are rigid. When I get used to such interaction, I will want to avoid the unpredictability of the other because I have become used to an other who fulfills my expectations. Confronting the other as a true subject with agency will become threatening because such an agentive subject will not be able to grant me the sort of recognition that I'm used to. It becomes more comfortable to interact with the other as an object that is under my own control. So I disregard the other-as-subject and represent her as an object in the psyche. In such a case, the self becomes swollen with objectifying representations of the other. And unfortunately, when my relation to the other resides mainly in intrapsychic space when faced with an other, then I will experience a sudden crisis whenever I am faced with the other in an intersubjective context. That is to say, when a relation is almost always as expected, it can be very startling for there to be unexpectedness all of the sudden. If the other acts in an unanticipated way, I may feel threatened because I do not anticipate her agency. In order not to feel threatened in this interchange, I will keep the other at bay, making sure that the recognition I receive is the sort that is comfortable for me, the sort that is static.

Conversely—and here is precisely where an extension of Freire's psychoanalytic work successfully departs from a liberal understanding of authority—it is also a mistake to be in an intersubjective circuit where the other is mainly unanticipatable. Such a relation also leads to domination. Let us say that the other resides mainly as *radically* other for me, that she is totally out of my control. Eventually, there will come a time when she seeks recognition from me. When I give recognition to an other who is unpredictable, to an other who does not represent for me some sort of stable image, then I will tend to give recognition that is random and subject to my own whims. That is to say, I must be able to see in the other some stable image, some specific other who needs recognition. If not, I will recognize randomly. In such a case of random recognition, the other will become subject to the vicissitudes of *my* unpredictability, to a randomness in recognizing that will be too unfamiliar to her. Even though I recognize the other, the recognition itself may be damaging in such an unpredictable case. Domination also results in such a case, when the other becomes dependent upon a recognitive encounter that cannot be anticipated because I can't be sure *whom* to recognize. Just opposite to the case where I cast the other in rigid terms and foist upon the other a recognition that is all my own, it is likewise dominating to be unpredictable in the granting of recognition. Such a situation also causes dependency on the one recognized.

DOMINATION AND SUBMISSION IN THE CLASSROOM

It is not hard to imagine such a relation of domination in the classroom. Let us say that I am a teacher and I know little about one of my students except what I can discern from his role *as my student*. This student certainly has a rich, unpredictable life that has little to do with what I know about him, but, nevertheless, I continue knowing this student only in the limited ways that he is permitted to interact with me within the particular parameters that I set up for the students in my class. Let us say that I keep the student in a banking relationship, and expect him to stay in such a role.

In such a relationship, it can be said that I have a relationship with that student that is based more on fantasy than on reality, more on the limited circumstances that I have predetermined while setting up my classroom than on the unpredictability and surprise that is part of human experience. In such a case, there will come a time that I give recognition to that student. In this case, the recognition that I give will tend to keep that student in his prescribed role. It will tend toward domination. I will give recognition from a perspective that is already dependent upon *me*. The other's recognition will be based on the "dependence that is the fruit of the concrete situation of domination," to borrow Freire's description. It will be based on the other's submission to my fantasy.

To put the issue of domination and submission in curricular terms, think of Freire's accusation that banking instructors separate instruction into two stages, the preparation and then the actual teaching. This sequential process is not itself the problem. To pretend that there will be absolutely no contemplation of curriculum "in the instructor's study or laboratory," is not, I believe, Freire's point.[34] His point is, rather, to note the long-term ill effects that such a process fosters. Such effects include domination on the part of the instructor, and submission on the part of the student. When instructors hide the preparation of content from students, the long-term effect of such hiding on the student is no different from the psychic process that leads to an imbalanced interchange between self and other. The instructor creates a rigid, preformulated curriculum. She creates a content that is solely under her control, one that is no different from an object of fantasy. In turn, the student must engage with this curriculum in the narrowly defined way that the instructor has prepared. The student, like the one dominated, must succumb to the objectifying grid

of the preset curriculum. He must fall in line with the narrow workings of the other's preformulated fantasy.[35]

In such a curricular situation, the student, trapped in a circuit of
succumbing to the fantasy-inspired curriculum of the instructor, has no
chance to become an agent in the learning process. If agency does take
place, if the student does engage with content *preparation*, then the
instructor is not in a position to recognize the student as having par-
taken in worthwhile learning.[36] In that case, the instructor, having become used to recognizing only that which she has formulated in advance,
will not recognize the validity of any learning that is not prepared under
her control. Agentive learning will not "count," as the instructor is able
to recognize only that learning which she has prearranged for the student. Curriculum will continue to be severed from its preparation because a cycle of domination and submission has set in.

Or, let us say that I am a teacher who "gives up authority." Let
us say I assume from the start that my student should not be the subject
of *my* understandings, that he should not be relegated to the student
roles I have in mind for him. That does not undo the scenario of
domination and submission; it only reverses its conditions. For, when I
"grant" autonomy, agency, and unpredictability to my student, there
will still come a time when the student seeks recognition from me. At
such a time, the recognition I grant him will be arbitrary because it will
be unpredictable. Ironically, my attempt to let the student free will make
him just as submissive to my whims as he was previously to my fantasy.

AUTHORITY AND BALANCE

Examined in light of intersubjective psychoanalysis, authority can neither be insisted on nor given up. Both stances will lead to domination
and submission. Rather, self and other must strike a balance where
acknowledgment is practiced on two levels: the level of fantasy and the
level of unpredictability. The challenge herein is to strike a balance that
takes into account both the strong need for recognition built into the
teacher/student relationship, *and* the omnipresent danger of becoming
entangled in circuits of recognition that are either dominating or submissive. The teacher/student relation has a natural tendency to fall into
stereotypical role playing that leads to domination and submission, *but*
the liberal eschewing of authority also leads down a similar path.

The way out of domination and submission is built on balance.
There must be a fluctuation in the self-other relation that at once encourages fantasy *and* reality. The teacher must be in a position to recognize the student as a separate center of self, one that is out of her own
control. However, for such recognition to count, the student cannot be

so far out of the teacher's control that she becomes a threat. There must be an oscillation, on the part of the teacher, between being in control and letting loose. And there must be such an oscillation on the side of the student, too. For recognition to count, the student must know that the teacher is predictable enough not to be threatening. Yet, the teacher must seem autonomous enough not to *have to* grant recognition. Recognition counts for the one recognized only when there is the option, on the part of the one recognizing, of not recognizing.

These psychoanalytic insights point precisely to what Freire is after when he argues that "authority must be *on the side of* freedom." To enhance freedom, authority must work against its own tendency to dominate the other. For authority to enhance freedom does not mean that it *is* freedom. It means rather that authority must be enacted more judiciously than has heretofore been considered. It must be deployed with an eye toward alleviating the bonds of domination and submission that characterize many educational interactions, and most oppressive situations.

For Freire, it is not authority that is the problem. The problem is rather the subservience that may result from authority that is exercised injudiciously. When Freire states that "arguments based on authority are no longer valid," this statement should *not* be read as a liberalist critique that assumes authority to be some problem in itself. Authority, without the concomitant subservience that sometimes results from its use, is no more of a problem in itself than the clanging piano is itself at fault for having been played awkwardly. Authority becomes a problem when it is used in ways that either rigidify the other or let the other loose completely. The judicious use of authority will strive to avoid the poles of dominance and submission. Its judicious use will subvert the banking tendency that employs authority to maintain the circuit of domination and submission. It is such a circuit, and not authority itself, that carries out the work of banking—producing passive students, precluding epistemological and existential agency, severing students from the production of knowledge, replicating dominant ideology, and installing the banking method in student consciousness.

Balance is as applicable to classroom authority as it is to psychic circuits of recognition. On the instructor's side, it is necessary to conscientiously allow for my own agency. There are certainly times when one must teach in the way one wants. But at the same time, it is necessary to realize that my position as educator must be tempered by the position of an other who is not under my control. For me to teach in a way that counts, I must stake out my own position, yet be willing to lose that position from time to time. Similarly, the student must be allowed by me to stake out her position, but must also be willing to lose that position from time to time. It is only by such a movement between the interior domain of one's own pedagogical agenda, and the exterior domain of the other's intellectual growth, that circuits of domination and submission will be kept at bay.

It will be argued at this point that I have started with the naïve reading of Freire, one that recommends giving up authority altogether, that I have made a detour through authority's relation to the psyche, and that I have merely come back to a more "balanced" approach to Freire, one that is ultimately not about the psychic dynamics of authority but more about some sort of "reasonable" conscious use of authority. I want to emphasize that this is not the case. When I advocate balance, I do not mean a happy medium where threat is avoided and the other remains within the realm of the anticipatable. I mean instead balance in the sense that a pendulum must be balanced, and not tilted to one side or the other, if it is to continue to oscillate. The circuit of recognition will entail oscillation. There will be times when authority seems uncontrollably lost, times when the other will seem to have taken over, times when the teacher, for instance, finds herself in a vulnerable position that threatens to engulf all reasonable progress within the classroom. Vulnerability will be inevitable. One cannot anticipate, with any accuracy, the times when the other will be unexpected and threatening. Authority without domination will oscillate toward vulnerability, and back again.

In short, authority must be seen as a dynamic and intersubjective process. When Freire describes an authority that enhances freedom, we must understand such authority in the same way that we understand the circuits of recognition that are fundamental to all self-other relations. Such authority does *not* enhance freedom when it gets stuck in an imbalance that leads to continued domination on the side of one person, and continued submission on the side of another. Such authority *does* enhance freedom when states of domination and submission are merely fleeting, fleeting to such an extent that they constitute momentary experiences of threat, vulnerability, omnipotence, and excess. During these moments, authority is at work in motion. It does not freeze into domination. Authority that enhances freedom is best judged by the extent to which vulnerability and excess are precisely *not* avoided. It can be judged by the extent to which vulnerability and excess are kept in motion, sometimes practiced by the self and sometimes by the other. This oscillation must never get stuck. Both teacher and students must practice excess. Both students and teachers must experience vulnerability.

Authority must be in flux, sometimes abdicated and sometimes claimed. It must be used, as Freire notes, so that "through dialogue, the teacher-of-the-students and the students-of-the-teacher cease to exist and a new term emerges: teacher-student with students-teachers."[37] It must be used on the fault line between fantasy and unexpectedness, between domination and submission, within the oscillation of excess and vulnerability, and thus "on the side of freedom."[38]

CONCLUSION

In this concluding chapter, I have ended up claiming something audacious. I have claimed that even the work of the great educator Paulo Freire stands to gain from a more thoroughly relational examination of authority. Indeed, this last chapter has been different from the rest. In this chapter I have tried to augment a long-standing educational program by using a relational approach to authority. In contrast, the preceding chapters have been more or less based on the *experience* of relational authority. I have examined the relation of authority between texts and people. I have examined the way that the relation of authority is like a literary relation. I have examined the relation of authority when the person in authority is no longer present. I have examined how one relates to larger, impersonal sources of authority. And I have examined how the authority relation bears on the use of questions. So instead of using relational authority to think through *experience*, this last chapter has used relational authority to think through a *theory*.

But to conclude this book, I would like to go back once again to lived experience. I would like to share just a few experiences from my own teaching and from my own life. I share these experiences in no particular order, yet they all have something in common. These reflections all invoke different insights to be gleaned from a relational perspective on authority. I trust that the reader of the pages that follow will be able to see how these reflections stem from the work that I have already done in the preceding chapters.

I leave these reflections for you to think about for this reason: if this book has done anything, it should have given the reader a way to understand authority differently. The ideas that have been put forth in this book should enable the reader to re-understand *any* instance when authority is in play. And so here I will offer just a few instances that come to mind. Here, I will be challenging myself to rethink a few instances of authority that I have come across. I do this because if one cannot rethink, in a relational way, *any and all* instances of authority, then the book fails. There should be no exception. After all, it is not just certain types of authority that are relational. *All* authority is so.

Recently I was teaching a graduate seminar on moral philosophy in education. We were discussing a passage in the book *I and Thou*, written by Martin Buber. Students were taking turns offering insights.

As one student offered comments, she used the pronoun "it" in a way that I did not understand. I asked her,

"What do you mean by 'it'? You used the word 'it' in your last sentence. I can't figure out what 'it' is referring to."

She replied, "I'm not sure what I mean."

Another student offered his comments. Once again, it happened. I interrupted him, asking, "Can you tell me what *you* mean by 'it'? As with Carol, I can't put my finger on the meaning of the word 'it' as you have used it."

He replied, "I think by the word 'it' I mean 'spirit' or 'language' or 'presence.' But I'm not positive."

I asked a third student for his insights because I could see in his eyes that he had something to say about the passage. He began to speak, but then stopped mid-sentence.

He said, "I don't know if I can go on with my idea because I was about to say 'it' and I know that you are going to ask me what 'it' means, and I don't know what the 'it' that I am going to say means.

At first I was frustrated that my previous questioning had caused a halt in the conversation. But then I smiled to myself because I realized that the questioning, and the halt, were very productive. This last interchange illustrates the way that authority can oscillate between teacher and student, especially when questions are asked by the teacher. Such oscillation is productive. It is important for questioning to exhibit reciprocity. In this instance, my student wobbled the box. He kept the dice rolling.

When the third student responded to me, he did not let himself be pigeon-holed by the question. Rather, he turned my question back onto me. He wondered what I intended by my question. He wondered if it was reasonable for me to come back at him with another question. He examined what the question might entail. He wondered, out loud, where I would be going with my question. He questioned my question. He turned my question into his own question. He caught *me* up short. He partook in the authority exchange rather than letting authority be a one-way relation.

Three years ago, my mother died. My mother was, quite simply, the most import figure of authority in my life. She was a moral authority for me. A social activist, she taught me to work against racism in all its forms. A white woman unafraid to go against the grain at a time when schools in many parts of the United States were segregated, she and a handful of other progessive, white parents had their children bussed into an all black elementary school. I was bussed to McCarver elementary school at the age of seven, and I will forever live by the anti-racist values that she embodies.

She was a pedagogical authority for me. My mother set a standard of teaching that I may never live up to, but will always strive to attain. She was not a teacher by profession. She did, though, have a teacherly way with people. One might call this way a matter of 'unconditional intellectual regard.' For my mother, the intellectual potential of her children was never to be challenged. Her children simply *could*. She let no one say differently. She let none of her children think otherwise.

Since she has passed away, I have come to know something I had never known before. My mother had all along been the authority figure to whom I had turned for guidance. It wasn't that I asked her in person for guidance, at least not after I became an adult. It was rather that she authorized me by being front-and-center in my memory, in my psyche. If I trained to run a marathon, I thought of my mother. If I attended a protest march, I thought of my mother. If I put on snow skis and skied gracefully down the hill, I thought of her smiling.

After she passed away, though, I must admit that her presence as an authority figure changed. I could no longer look to her without grief overshadowing. Try as I might, I could no longer look to her with the hope that she would authorize me in person. She was no longer the same sort of living authority. She is, and will always be, central to who I am. Yet, I have learned that I must look to others as well. My father is still alive and flourishing. He is slowly insinuating himself into that position of authority that my mother can now only hold in a certain way. He is becoming my living absence. Through this transition, it has helped me to know that authority is a relation. It has helped me to know that authority is a relation that depends upon presence as well as absence.

The reasons that I have written this book are many. One of them stems from interactions that I have had with university colleagues. If you learn anything as a university professor, it is that authority is always at stake when colleagues get together. This is in part because of the hierarchical nature of academic life. Academics are *always* being ranked in one way or another whether it is by one's scholarship, one's teaching ability, or, as in the case I want to recount, one's racial identity. Who gets authorized when professors have the occasion speak with each other is always a matter of tension. One specific occasion comes to mind.

At the university where I used to work, our college of education was replete with racial tension. African American and Latino faculty members were subject to personal and institutional racism. For example, one Latina faculty member, mistaken for a student worker because most of the student workers in our faculty were Latino, was asked by a white faculty member to make photocopies. Too, some white members of the faculty would complain when one African American faculty member, in particular, would speak out, when she would speak her mind. Some white members of the faculty accused her of bullying white women. Race was used as a wedge by some white faculty members to mark off those who had a right to speak out and those who didn't. Of course, the white accusers were the first to defend their own right to speak as forcefully as they wished.

Adding to the racial tension was a refusal by some white members of our faculty to acknowledge that significant racial tension *existed*. To them, racial tension among faculty members was a thing that should never be confused with the "real" racism that happens in less rarefied situations outside of academia. To them, "real" racism did not happen where people of color had already achieved an academic position of authority.

To make a long story short, the tension was so extreme that an outside consultant was called in by our dean. This consultant recommended that all faculty members participate in workshops to understand, and to talk about, the racism that was being experienced. I was asked by the dean to lead these workshops. The reason I was asked to do so was that I was seen as a white person who would not appear to represent one side or the other in any partisan way. Another way of saying this is that I was asked to lead these workshops because, if an African American person was leading them, then the authority of that person might have been undermined by a presumed bias. The dean told me that I had a certain authority enabling me to conduct this particular set of workshops. I "had" authority because of my whiteness.

Looking back on this experience, I now have a different understanding of the way that authority got enacted, through me, during these workshops. For, the reason that I was able to assume a place of authority is not *simply* because I was white. Indeed, some white folks on faculty would not have been able to assume such a place because they enacted a white identity that had already offended others. They would not have been able to assume such a place because they were the ones who had been accused of racism. Other white folks on faculty would not have been able to assume such a place because they had enacted a white identity that clearly sided with folks of color who had been the target of racism. In my case, it just happened that I was in a relational position, a position that happened to straddle, and, yes, have affinities with, both those who were offended and those who did the offending. It wasn't that I was white, nor was it that I had some "true" position, some "true" knowledge that enabled me to conduct these workshops. It was rather that I had a tenable *relation* with both factions. It was the relation itself that authorized me.

Throughout the writing of this book, I have had the unique opportunity to teach a large lecture class entitled "Education and Social

Issues." This opportunity has been unique in that it has challenged most of my prior assumptions about authority. In the past, I had always assumed that lecturing to ninety students entailed an unreasonable imposition of authority. After all, I have considered myself to be a progressive educator. Along with Paulo Freire, I have assumed that lecturing *to* students indicates a certain "narrative sickness."[39] I have assumed that dialogue *with* and *among* students is the preferable means of communication. Certainly, it is very difficult to have dialogue with as many as ninety interlocutors.

Yet, throughout these years of lecturing, I have also been struck by a certain paradox that puts into question the simple assumption that lecturing is a *wrong* imposition of authority. The paradox is this: On the one hand, I have felt uncomfortable lecturing to a large audience of students. I have felt uncomfortable because of the "banking method" that it entails. On the other hand, I have long enjoyed attending poetry readings. Often sitting in theatre audiences that have been even larger than the audience of my students in lecture class, I have enjoyed hearing the spoken word, the word of poetry, flowing from a poet on stage. It has long seemed paradoxical to me that I have not felt dominated or "banked" at poetry readings.[40] Yet at the same time, I have felt that my own lecturing to a large audience has been too much of an authoritarian imposition. I have wondered what the difference between a poetry reading and a lecture really is. Is there any difference at all?

During the first couple years of my lecture class, I figured that the only way for me to become more progressive in my pedagogy was to create dialogue in this large lecture setting. I created opportunities for my students to talk among themselves. I asked students to work in small groups to discuss the readings that had been assigned. I did everything I could to let students speak in class. Meanwhile, though, the authoritative paradox of the poetry reading continued to bother me. Why couldn't I be the poet? I often asked myself. Why is *my* authority so intrusive while the poet's is not?

More recently, I must admit that I have given up somewhat on my efforts to let student dialogue guide the flow of my lecture class. Quite simply, these efforts proved to be strained. Though I created the opportunity for students to talk among themselves in small groups, the students often remarked that such times were not very productive. While I took great pains to recreate the atmosphere of a more intimate dialogue, this large lecture setting hasn't allowed for true dialogue of the sort that is clearly attainable in smaller settings. I have found that one can't use a progressive template for pedagogy anywhere and everywhere.

In fact, I have now come to a different understanding of authority in this lecture class. I now lecture to this large group of students unabashedly. I have found that students are more profoundly moved by the spoken word of the lecture. I have found that students engage more deeply with the concepts presented. When students come to visit me in my office, or when we talk in the halls, they have more to say than before. Interestingly, the dialogue that we *do* have with each other is now less frequent, but is also more substantial. Students speak up in class in ways that didn't happen previously. They challenge my position right there in front of so many of their peers. They speak their minds. I listen. I do not need to be imposing about what I present in class. It is there for the taking, or for the walking away. At least this is my interpretation of what has happened as the years have progressed.

Now, I am not claiming to have become the poet. But the lesson of the literary relation is germane here. I am convinced that the relation of authority must be considered in a literary light. Even the authority relation establish by a professor in a large lecture class. I read my failure to successfully import progressive methodology as a comment on the literary life of authority. The quality of the authority relation, I would now say, never depends solely on some fixed method, just as the quality of a literary work never depends solely on some fixed style. A certain progressive methodology may facilitate a healthy authority relation, but it may not. In the same way, a certain free verse form of poetry may authorize the work of a poet, but it may not. The authority relation between teacher and student will benefit from different forms at different times. In this particular situation, I have found that the speaking voice of the teacher is the form of choice.

I would like to further explore the literary life of authority, the one outlined in chapter 2, with the following example.

One of the courses that PhD students are required to take in my department focuses on the history of educational thought. In this course, students are asked to read a series of texts considered to be canonical in Western education. They read Plato, John Locke, Jean-Jacques Rousseau, Mary Wollstonecraft, and John Dewey, among others. The aim of this course, as stated the course syllabus, is "to consider the major contributions to educational theory in their historical contexts."

Certainly, this list of authors raises profound questions about authority. And of course, such questions have already garnered lots of air time in academic discussions over the past decades. Questions such as the following arise: Who "has" the authority to say that these texts are "the major contributions"? Do these texts deserve the ("thingified") authority that is attributed to them? Which groups of people benefit from the ("thingified") authority that is attributed to these texts? Which types of education are authorized by such texts? Which types are not?

Though I have never taught this course, I have had the opportunity to talk with many students who have taken it. These students have had various reactions to the course and its content. Some, like Judith, have had a very positive reaction. She has related to me what a profoundly moving experience it has been to engage with these canonical authors. For Judith, her understanding of educational thought has been greatly enlarged because she can now pinpoint where competing conceptions of educational thought in the West originate. She is happy to know where the current debates over educational practices reside on a larger plain of various intellectual traditions.

For others such as Stephen, this course has been worthless. For him, this investigation of Western educational origins is just another exercise in the performance of hegemony. He would rather that we, as educators, move on. He has had enough of exploring a canon that has served to segregate and oppress.

I have also listened to professors and students who say they are tired of complaints such as Stephen's. Stephen is dismissed as being anti-intellectual, as being unwilling to engage in the intellectual work of learning from history. It is this dismissal of Stephen's perspective that I would like to look at more closely.

With the literary life of authority in mind, I find it difficult to jump to the conclusion that Stephen should be written off as anti-intellectual. For, such a writing-off entails a mistaken focus on content. Such a writing-off assumes that these canonical texts are somehow self-authorizing. It assumes that such works should be automatically authorized because of the rich content that they offer. Certainly, the content of Plato's *Republic* and the content of Emile's *Rousseau* are rich. About this there can be no question. The question is, rather, whether we can ever assume that content per se is sufficient for authority to gain purchase within the educational relation. The relation of authority depends not only upon content. It depends as well upon how things are taught, and who is doing the teaching.

Indeed, no work will ever authorize itself simply because it has a lot to say. This is true of classroom content just as it is true of great literary works. In education, content alone does not "have" authority. Instead, there will always be an interplay between three things: the way the text is presented, the content of the text, and the authority enacted by the instructor. All three of these variables will come into play when students read a classroom text. Students' involvement in the authority relation depends upon a combination of style, content, and personhood. Stephen may not be correct in dismissing these rich texts wholesale. However, the fact remains that the content of these texts may not suffice to bring him into an educative relation with authority. Sometimes, texts do not speak for themselves.

My daughter Olivia is now ten years old. She has started at a new school this year. At this new school, there has been an interesting shift in her confidence at mathematics. Whereas last year she didn't fair too well at mathematics, this year things are different. This year she will tell you that mathematics is her favorite subject. Last year, math was a distant last on her list of favorite subjects. At this new school, Olivia considers herself an authority at mathematics.

Having talked to Olivia about this newfound interest in math, I think I can pinpoint the time when things changed for her. It was on a day when the students in Olivia's class were doing what I call "long-multiplication"—multiplying multidigit numbers together. Olivia's teacher noticed that Olivia was using a different algorithm than the rest of the students in her class.

Olivia's teacher approached her and asked, "Olivia, will you show me the way you are doing your multiplication?"

"Yes," Olivia responded, "I do it like this. . . ." She showed the teacher her process.

"That's the old-fashioned algorithm, Olivia. That's exactly what I'm trying to teach to our class this year. Last year they used the new math algorithm, but the old-fashioned one is better. That's why I want all the kids learn your way.

Olivia, can you be our tutor this year? Can you help students who don't know your way of multiplying?"

"I can do that," Olivia responded.

Olivia tells this story with pride, and, yes, with authority. In my mind, this story points to one thing. It points to a new *relation* of authority, a relation that has authorized Olivia to be an expert at mathematics. It is not that a lightbulb suddenly went on this year in Olivia's mathematical mind. It is not that Olivia didn't "have" authority last year, but "has" it this year. After all, what Olivia "had" last year was exactly what she "has" this year, namely, a certain ability to do the long multiplication the old-fashioned way. It is the relation that has changed. Olivia's teacher was able to facilitate a relation between Olivia and her peers that put her in a place of authority.

I have offered here just a few examples from my own experience, and I have tried to think through them keeping in mind that authority is a relation. As it turns out, it is not difficult to think of authority in terms of relation. However, it still proves easy to fall back into the habit of thinking of authority as a thing, as a substance. It is a fact that each of the experiences above could be reframed in terms of who "had" authority, and what he or she did with that authority that he or she "had." Yet, I am hoping that this book has provided enough evidence to convince its readers not to fall back into the habit of treating authority as a substance. Authority is a relation. The evidence attests to this fact. If we continue to treat authority as a substance, it is a matter of habit rather than a matter of accuracy.

Notes

INTRODUCTION

1. Here I use the term *folk notion* to refer to a commonplace, widely accepted conception that gets used without questioning the presumptions of such a conception.

2. See Ira Shor, *Empowering Education : Critical Teaching for Social Change* (Chicago: University of Chicago Press, 1992); and *Critical Teaching and Everyday Life* (Chicago: University of Chicago Press, 1987).

3. See E. D. Hirsch, *The Schools We Need and Why We Don't Have Them* (New York: Anchor Books, 1999); Diane Ravitch, *The Schools We Deserve* (New York: Basic Books, 1985).

4. See Henry Giroux, "Authority, Intellectuals, and the Politics of Practical Learning," *Teachers College Record* 88, 1 (Fall 1986): 22–40; *Pedagogy and the Politics of Hope* (Boulder: Westview, 1997); *Schooling and the Struggle for Public Life* (Minneapolis: University of Minnesota Press, 1998).

5. Immanuel Kant, "What Is Enlightenment?" http://www.fordham.edu/halsall/mod/kant-whatis.html (Oct 2, 2005).

6. Paulo Freire, *Pedagogy of the Oppressed* (New York: Continuum, 1970).

7. Ibid., 61.

8. Louis Althusser, "Ideology and Ideological State Apparatuses (Notes toward an Investigation)," in Slavoj Zizek, *Mapping Ideology* (New York: Verso Press, 1994), 100–40.

9. Ibid., 31.

10. Franz Fanon, *Black Skins/White Masks*, trans. Charles Lam Markmann (New York: Grove Press, 1967), 109.

11. Michel Foucault, *The Foucault Reader*, ed. Paul Rabinow (New York: Pantheon Books, 1984), 61.

12. Ibid., 49.

CHAPTER 1. TEXTS AND THE AUTHORITY RELATION

1. The works I rely on here are Hans-Georg Gadamer, *Truth and Method* (New York: Continuum Books, 1995); *The Enigma of Health* (London: Polity

Press, 1996); and Jacques Derrida, *Of Grammatology*, trans. Gayatri Chakravorty Spivak (Baltimore: The Johns Hopkins University Press, 1974).

2. Athol Fugard, *My Children! My Africa!* (New York: Theatre Communications Group, 1989).

3. Ibid., 279.

4. Gadamer, *Enigma*, 119.

5. Gadamer, *Truth and Method*, 278.

6. See Jacques Derrida's discussion of supplementarity in *Of Grammatology*, 144–47. See also Charles Bingham, "I Am the Missing Pages of the Text I Teach: Gadamer and Derrida on Teacher Authority," *Philosophy of Education 2001* (Urbana-Champaign: Philosophy of Education Society, 2002), 265–72.

7. Derrida, *Of Grammatology*, 144–45.

8. Ibid., 145.

9. Ibid., 146.

10. Ibid., 146–47.

11. Toni Morrison, *Playing in the Dark: Whiteness and the Literary Imagination* (New York: Vintage, 1993).

12. See J. L. Austin, *How to Do Things with Words* (Cambridge: Harvard University Press, 1975).

13. Athol Fugard, *My Children! My Africa!* (Theater Communications Group, 1990).

14. Ibid., 67–68.

15. Ibid.

16. Ibid., 63–64.

17. Ibid., 24.

18. Ibid., 43.

19. Ibid., 23–24.

20. Ibid., 25.

21. Ibid., 43.

CHAPTER 2. THE LITERARY RELATION OF AUTHORITY

1. In Jacques Derrida, "Before the Law," in *Acts of Literature*, ed. Derek Attridge (New York: Routledge, 1992), 183, 184.

2. Ibid., 183.

3. Ibid., 184.

4. Franz Kafka, *The Metamorphosis, In the Penal Colony, and Other Stories*, trans. Willa and Edwin Muir (New York: Schocken, 1995); *The Castle*, trans. Mark Harman (New York: Schocken, 1998); *The Trial*, trans. Willa and Edwin Muir (New York: Schocken, 1984).

5. See Eric L. Santner, *On the Psychotheology of Everyday Life: Reflections on Freud and Rosenweig* (Chicago: University of Chicago Press, 2001), 40.

6. Plato, *Meno*, trans. G. M. A. Grube (Indianapolis: Hackett, 1976).

7. Plato, *The Last Days of Socrates: Euthyphro; The Apology; Creto; Phaedo* (New York: Penguin Classics, 1993).

8. Anamnesis refers to the Greek belief that human beings share a collective memory.

9. Derrida, "Before the Law," 213.

10. Ibid., 213.

11. Ibid., 196.

12. Ibid., 204.

13. I would like to thank reviewers at the *Journal of Philosophy of Education* for pointing this out.

14. John Stewart, ed., *Beyond the Symbol Model* (Albany: State University of New York Press, 1996), 20.

15. George Lakoff and Mark Taylor, *Metaphors We Live By* (Chicago: University of Chicago Press, 2003), 10.

16. Ibid., 11.

17. Stewart, *Beyond the Symbol Model*, 20.

18. Alphonso Lingis, *The Community of Those Who Have Nothing in Common* (Indianapolis: University of Indiana Press, 1994).

19. Ibid., 4.

20. Gadamer, *Truth and Method*, 268–69.

21. Austin, *How to Do Things With Words*. Austin does not even entertain the notion that same-sex couples can marry, too.

22. Ibid.

23. Santner, *Psychopathology*, 133. By "constative," Santner means the ordinary decoding of the literal meaning of a passage. By "redemptive," Santner means the religiously transformative reading of a passage.

24. Ibid., 133.

CHAPTER 3. RELATING TO AUTHORITY
FIGURES WHO ARE NOT THERE

1. Here I am again referring to mainstream educational accounts of authority, be they progressive, traditional, or critical, accounts that include: Kenneth Benne, "The Locus of Educational Authority in Today's World," *Teachers College Record* 88, 1 (Fall 1986): 15–21; Giroux, "Authority"; Patricia White, "Self-respect, Self-esteem, and the School: A Democratic Perspective on Authority," *Teachers College Record* 88, 1 (Fall 1986): 95–106; Emily Robertson, "Teacher Authority and Teaching for Liberation," *Philosophy of Education Society*, 1994, <http://www.ed.uiuc.edu/eps/ pes~yearbook/ 94_docs/roberso.htm> (June 10, 2000); Edward Sankowski, "Autonomy, Education, and Politics," *Philosophy of Education Society*, <http://www.ed.uiuc.edu/eps/pes~yearbook/ 1998/sankowski.html> (July 15, 2000).

2. See Jean Laplance and J. B. Pontalis, *The Language of Psycho-Analysis* (New York: W.W. Norton, 1974).

3. See Jessica Benjamin, *The Bonds of Love: Psychoanalysis, Feminism, and the Problem of Domination* (New York: Pantheon, 1988); *Like Subjects, Love Objects: Essays on Recognition and Social Difference* (New Haven: Yale

University Press, 1995); and *Shadow of the Other: Intersubjectivity and Gender in Psychoanalysis* (New York: Routledge, 1998).

4. Benjamin, *Bonds of Love*, 30.

5. Ibid., 31.

6. Ibid., 19ff.

7. Benjamin, *Like Subjects*, 30.

8. Benjamin, *Bonds of Love*, 43.

9. See John Dewey, *Experience and Education* (New York: Collier Books, 1963).

10. Edmund Husserl, *Cartesian Meditations*, trans. Dorian Cairns (The Hague: Martinus Nijhoff, 1970), 112–13.

11. For comments on this apperceptive process, see Kathleen M. Haney, *Intersubjectivity Revisited: Phenomenology and the Other* (Athens: Ohio University Press, 1994), 57–60.

12. Husserl, *Meditations*, 112.

13. Maurice Merleau-Ponty, *Phenomenology, Language, and Sociology: Selected Essays of Maurice Merleau-Ponty*, ed. John O'Neill (London: Heinemann, 1974), 81–94.

14. Ibid., 81–94.

15. Ibid.

16. Ibid., p. 91. Please notice that while this aspect of language sounds a bit similar to the sender-receiver model it is actually quite different insofar as language is not considered a neutral vehicle for the transfer of ideas but rather a uniquely linguistic medium that actually comes alive through the act of human communication.

17. Benjamin, *Like Subjects*, 30.

18. Ibid., 202–205; Benjamin, *Shadow of the Other*, 25–30.

19. Here, I am entering a contentious conversation about the more general question of whether or not language is a symbolic system. My position on this is as follows: language does make use of symbols, but it does so in a *functional, living* way. There are two points that I am trying trying to make here. First, I do not consider language to be a symbolic system, per se. That is to say, I do not consider language to be *only* a symbolic system. Language certainly acts in other nonsymbolic ways as well. Second, I do not consider language's use of symbols to be a use of "just" symbols in the sense that symbols are construed of as a lesser order of things, as an order of things that is somehow ontologically distinct and less important than things in the "real" world. Rather, language's symbols are part and parcel of the same real world where everything else resides. Language may use symbols, but these symbols are not lesser or greater, in fact have no ontological distinction, from the "real world" itself. For an introduction to this contentious debate, please see Stewart, ed., *Beyond the Symbol Model*; and John Stewart, *Language as Articulate Contact: Towards a Post-Semiotic Philosophy of Language* (Albany: State University of New York Press, 1995).

20. Benjamin, *Shadow of the Other*, 28.

21. Benjamin, *Like Subjects*, 202.

CHAPTER 4. WHEN FACED WITH AUTHORITY

1. See, for example, Alexander Nehemas, *The Art of Living* (Berkeley: University of California Press, 1998); Pierre Hadot, *Philosophy as a Way of Life*, ed. Arnold Davidson (Cambridge: Blackwell, 1995); and Michel Foucault, *Technologies of the Self: A Seminar with Michel Foucault*, ed. Luther H. Martin, Huck Gutman, and Patrick H. Hutton (Amherst: University of Massachusetts Press, 1988).

2. I take this phrase from Richard Rorty's *The Consequences of Pragmatism* (Minneapolis: University of Minnesota Press, 1982).

3. See Dewey, *Experience and Education*.

4. Ibid., 27–28.

5. Immanuel Kant, *Foundations of the Metaphysics of Morals* (New York: The Liberal Arts Press, 1959), 47–49.

6. Kant, "What is Enlightenment?"

7. Friedrich Nietzsche, *On the Genealogy of Morals* (New York: Vintage Books, 1967), 59.

8. Nietzsche, *Genealogy*.

9. Ibid., 59.

10. Here I am referring to the following texts by Foucault: "bio-power," in *History of Sexuality Vol. I: An Introduction* (New York: Pantheon, 1978); "surveillance" and "confessional techniques," in *Discipline and Punish: The Birth of the Prison* (New York: Pantheon, 1977); "epistemic regimes," in *The Order of Things: An Archaeology of the Human Sciences* (New York: Pantheon, 1971); and "governmental hierarchies," in *Technologies of the Self*.

11. Michel Foucault, *Power/Knowledge: Selected Interviews and Other Writings 1972–1977* (New York: Pantheon, 1980), 74.

12. For a discussion on Winnicott's anti-Kantian stance, see Barbara Johnson, "Using People: Kant with Winnicott," in *The Turn to Ethics*, ed. Marjorie Garber, Beatrice Hanssen, Rebecca L. Walkowitz (New York: Routledge, 2000), 47–63.

13. See D. W. Winnicott, *Playing and Reality* (New York: Routledge, 1971).

14. Certainly, my account of Winnicottian "use" does not do justice to the overall psychoanalytic territory that Winnicott establishes through his analysis of using, destruction, survival, relating, play, potential space, transitional space, transitional objects, etc. That is to say, I have isolated the phenomenon of "use" without giving a proper account of the way that use is but a small part of a larger constellation of processes contributing to the psychic flourishing of individuals. This omission is carried out intentionally on the assumption that Winnicott's understanding of psychic flourishing is implied, even if not theoretically elaborated, in this chapter on using others. This chapter focuses not on the psychic life of using others, but on its conscious life. By omitting the unconscious thrust of Winnicott's work in this chapter, I am not trying to say that the psychic life of using others is not important, but that an analysis of the use of authority can cover important ground even before it gets to the more nuanced elements of psychic life.

15. *Playing*, 111 ff.

16. Once again, I am echoing the work of Alexander Nehemas, among others. See note 1 of this chapter.

17. See Kieran Egan, *The Educated Mind: How Cognitive Tools Shape Our Understanding* (Chicago: University of Chicago Press, 1997).

18. Nehemas, *The Art of Living*, 4.

19. Nietzsche, *Genealogy*, 45.

20. Friedrich Nietzsche, *Ecce Homo*, trans. Walter Kaufman (New York: Vintage Books, 1967), 224–25.

21. Ibid., 282.

22. Friedrich Nietzsche, "Schopenhauer as Educator," in *Unfashionable Observations*, ed. Ernst Behler (Stanford: Stanford University Press, 1995), 171–255.

23. Nietzsche, *Ecce Homo*, 277.

24. Ibid., 277.

25. Ibid., 258.

26. See Nietzsche, *Ecce Homo*, "Zarathustra," and *The Gay Science*, trans. Walter Kaufmann (New York: Vintage Books, 1974), 270.

27. Nietzsche, *Genealogy*, 15.

28. Friedrich Nietzsche, *Beyond Good and Evil*, trans. Walter Kaufman (New York: Vintage Books, 1966), 127.

29. Nietzsche, *Genealogy*, 15.

30. Ibid., 39.

31. Ibid.

32. Here I think of intelligence tests, career inventories, and all sorts of other tests that claim to make assessments of one's "natural" abilities and aptitudes. There is a loathesome, and fundamentally uneducative, result when one takes only this first step, when one assumes that such measures actually indicate what one has the capacity to do and what one does not.

33. Of course, it is important to recall that whatever seems "natural" in education may in fact be a human invention. Michel Foucault's work on prisons, asylums, military barracks, medical discourses, and schools has shown very clearly the powers that institutions such as schools have to shape the self, to make students into "docile bodies." As he reminds us, systems of power have their own ways of making us believe that this or that is "natural" to you or me. One such system is the discourse of psychology. Restrictive yet ubiquitous psychological discourses dominate human practices these days. They especially dominate educational practices.

Yet even if the natural is a human invention, such an invention can be a venue for self-fashioning and for human flourishing. For Foucault, the act of self-fashioning serves to mitigate against scientist labeling, against statistical categorizing, against medicalizations of all kinds. He insists, especially in his later work, that self-fashioning can be a strategy toward whatever is deemed "natural" by power. He reminds us that self-fashioning is a way of refusing to be dominated, in this modern culture of ours, by systems of disciplinary power that tend to offer us limitations rather than freedoms. And, he reminds us that while power is indeed ubiquitous, it also produces its own resistances. Sites of power also produce sites that can effectively resist that power. Thus, for Foucault, we can use tactics of resistance precisely where power resides. With regard to the specific sorts of power mechanisms that one finds in institutions such as schools, mechanisms that produce docile, "natural" selves, it is not unreasonable to find in those same institutions sites for resisting the production of docile bodies. Self-fashioning is a strategy of resistance best practiced in the very places where "natural" selves are produced, in places such as schools.

34. Nietzsche, *Genealogy*, 15.

35. With Socrates' claim that he is the one who knows he does not know, with Montaigne's suggestion that the educated child should be "well-formed" instead of "well-filled," and with Foucault's practical return to the care of the self in his later work, we find a willingness to limit oneself when it comes to knowledge. See Michel de Montaigne's "On the Education of Children," in *Selected Essays*, ed. Blanchard Bates (New York: The Modern Library, 1949); David Hansen, "Well-Formed, Not Well-Filled: Montaigne and the Paths of Personhood," *Educational Theory* 52, 2 (Spring 2002); Michel Foucault, *The Use of Pleasure: The History of Sexuality, Volume 2*, trans. Robert Hurley (New York: Vintage Books, 1990); and *Technologies of the Self: A Seminar with Michel Foucault*.

36. Foucault, *History of Sexuality Vol. 2*, 7.

37. For a good essay on how Foucault changed his thinking, see John Rajchman, *Michel Foucault: The Freedom of Philosophy* (New York: Columbia University Press, 1986).

38. Foucault, *Technologies of the Self*, 9.

39. I have been advocating a philosophy of self-fashioning as a way to deal with the tensions that arise in education from the inevitable, and potentially contradictory, matters of nature, culture, and knowledge. To be sure, this investigation has not looked at enough of Nietzsche's thought with regard to these matters, nor has it investigated other self-fashioning philosophers such as Socrates and Montaigne who have much to teach us on these matters. But the aim here is not to exhaustively detail the natural, cultural, and epistemological insights that self-fashioning offers, but rather to identify a strand of thought that deserves to be explored further in the future. The aim of this investigation is to show that the trajectory of self-fashioning, a trajectory has been most thoroughly explored so far by Alexander Nehamas and Pierre Hadot, is perhaps the most important one that exists when it comes to the major problems that education poses. See especially Alexander Nehemas, *The Art of Living*; and, Pierre Hadot, *Philosophy as a Way of Life*.

Certainly, many have written on the educational insights to be gleaned from the various philosophers who happen to be philosophers of self-fashioning. But I am trying to foreground the educational significance of self-fashioning thought itself, rather than the specific thought of a Nietzsche or a Foucault per se. Clearly, this general approach to the theme of self-fashioning will not satisfy readers who want a detailed study of Nietzschean self-consitution, and Foucaultian agency, in education. For more detailed work on these educational matters I recommend my article "What Friedrich Nietzsche Cannot Stand About Education: Toward a Pedagogy of Self-Reformulation," *Educational Theory* 51,

3, as well as Chris Mayo's "The Uses of Foucault," *Educational Theory* 50, 1: 103–16.

CHAPTER 5. QUESTIONING AUTHORITY

1. Gadamer, *Truth and Method*, 375.
2. Ibid., 362.
3. Ibid., 262.
4. Ibid., 363.
5. Ibid.
6. Ibid., 362.
7. Ibid., 363.
8. Ibid.
9. Ibid.
10. Ibid.
11. See Heidegger's "Letter on Humanism," in *Martin Heidegger: Basic Writings, Second Edition* (San Francisco: Harper, 1993).
12. Gadamer, *Truth and Method*, 446.
13. See Gilles Deleuze, *Nietzsche and Philosophy*, trans. Hugh Tomlinson (New York: Columbia University Press, 1983).
14. Ibid., 474.
15. Ibid.
16. Hans-Georg Gadamer, *Philosophical Hermeneutics* (Berkeley: University of California Press, 1976), 35.
17. Gadamer, *Truth and Method*, 262–63.
18. Ibid., 263.
19. Ibid.
20. Here I am referring to Dewey's discussion in *The Child and Curriculum* (Chicago: University of Chicago Press, 1990), where he notes that the teacher must be concerned "with the subject matter as a related factor in a total and growing experience. Thus to see it is to psychologize it. It is the failure [of the teacher] to keep in mind the double aspect of subject matter which causes the curriculum and child to be set over against each other . . ." 201.
21. Gadamer, *Truth and Method*, 299.
22. Ibid.
23. Ibid., 375.
24. Freire, *Pedagogy of the Oppressed*, 72.

CHAPTER 6. PAULO FREIRE AND RELATIONAL AUTHORITY

1. Freire, *Pedagogy of the Oppressed*, 61.
2. Certainly, the problem of authority is of central concern to many versions of psychoanalysis. Such fundamental concepts of psychoanalysis as transference, the Oedipus complex, and shame are tied to issues of authority. And more specifically, the problem of authority within educational contexts has been written about in very interesting ways as of late. For examples of works

that address the interconnection of psychoanalysis, authority, and education, see especially Deborah Britzman's *Lost Subjects, Contested Objects: Toward a Psychoanalytic Inquiry of Learning* (Albany: State University of New York Press, 1999); Shoshona Felman's *Jacques Lacan and the Adventure of Insight: Psychoanalysis in Contemporary Culture* (Cambridge: Harvard University Press, 1987); and Appel's recent edited volume, *Psychoanalysis and Pedagogy* (New York: Bergin and Garvey, 1999). My concern in this essay is not, however, to explore the various understandings of authority, and more specifically educational authority, that have been analyzed in the literature of psychoanalysis. It is rather to take a particular version of psychoanalysis, one that is particularly suited to understanding Freire's work on authority, namely, Jessica Benjamin's intersubjective version, and to use it to understand his claims about how a liberatory authority might be configured.

I thus situate this chapter at the intersection of mainstream Freirean-inspired versions of critical pedagogy whose main proponent I consider to be Ira Shor (1987, 1992, 1996) on the one hand; and, on the other, those works cited above whose authors argue that psychoanalysis needs to inform the intersubjective dynamics of pedagogy. Ira Shor gives us very useful ways to employ Freirean pedagogy, but Jessica Benjamin's work lends further insight to the matter of critical authority.

   3. Freire, *Pedagogy of the Oppressed*, 54.
   4. Ibid., 56.
   5. Ibid., 61.
   6. Ibid., 64.
   7. Ibid.
   8. Ibid.
   9. Ibid., 68.
  10. Ibid., 176.
  11. Ibid.
  12. Ibid., 31.
  13. Ibid.
  14. Ibid., 54.
  15. John Dewey, "Authority and Social Change," in *Authority and the Individual* (Cambridge: Harvard University Press, 1937).
  16. Ibid., 171.
  17. Ibid., 177–78.
  18. Freire, *Pedagogy*, 60–61.
  19. At this point, it is important for me to state my assumptions about epistemology vis-à-vis intersubjectivity in Freire. I take Freire to be very psychoanalytic in his understanding of epistemology. Thus, when Freire mentions that we are "cognitive actors" who share the same "cognizable object," I take him to mean that cognition is a means by which intersubjective relations get worked out. It is not clear to me that Freire works out the link between epistemology and intersubjectivity adequately. Hence, this essay. I thus locate Freire within the sorts of psychoanalytic thinking typified by D. W. Winnicott and Jessica Benjamin that points out the ways humans interact by means of

object relations, "cognizable object" relations. See, for example, Winnicott's *Playing and Reality*.

20. Freire, *Pedagogy*, 61.

21. Here I am referring to the Enlightenment version of authority that Kant introduces in his essay, "What Is Enlightenment." Therein, Kant argues that freedom and authority are at odds. He argues that one must have the audacity to use one's own reason in the face of authority. It is this understanding of freedom versus authority that I am also calling a "liberal" version, liberalism being broadly defined as the intersection of discourses that advocate individualism and the separation of private and public spheres, such advocacy being glued together by the assumption that authority is contrary to individual freedom.

22. Michel Foucault, "What is Enlightenment?" in *Michel Foucault: Ethics, Subjectivity, and Truth*, ed. Paul Rabinow (New York: The New Press, 1997), 312.

23. Freire, *Pedagogy*, 67.

24. Ibid., 136.

25. Ibid., 137.

26. While this essay addresses primarily the recognitive implications of Freire's work, I have elsewhere argued for the centrality of recognition in all of education. Please see Charles Bingham, *Schools of Recognition: Identity Practices and Classroom Practices* (Boulder: Rowman and Littlefield, 2001).

27. Jessica Benjamin, *The Bonds of Love* (New York: Pantheon, 1988), 20–21.

28. Freire, *Pedagogy*, 58.

29. Ibid.

30. Benjamin, *Like Subjects*, 30.

31. Freire, *Pedagogy*, 148.

32. Ibid.

33. Maurice Freedman, *The Confirmation of Otherness: In Family, Community, and Society* (New York: Pilgrim Press, 1973), 30.

34. Freire, *Pedagogy*, 61.

35. Since I am speaking here in terms of "fantasy" versus "reality," it is appropriate to point out now that this distinction is properly a psychoanalytic one. It might be argued, in a philosophical critique of this essay, that I have not made a proper distinction between the two. I would not respond to such a critique, though. This distinction is rather a matter of discursive suppositions. It is a primary supposition of psychoanalysis that there is such a distinction, and that is one of the suppositions upon which this psychoanalytic augmentation of Freire is based.

36. Certainly there are a wide variety of ways in which students might engage in content preparation, some being pedagogically successful and some not. I am not trying to say that all content preparation is fortuitous, but am rather taking the case where such preparation *is* successful in order to think through the psychic dynamics of authority.

37. Friere, *Pedagogy*, 61.

38. I am grateful to the thoughtful comments and stimulating conversation of Michael Dupuis, James Fusco, Felicia Michaels, and Stephen Haymes, who helped me during the preparation of this chapter.

39. Freire, *Pedagogy*, 51.

40. Here I am referring once again to the work of Paulo Freire. I am referring to the "banking system of education" that narrates whatever it wants to the student who is to be "filled" with knowledge of the teacher's choice.

References

Althusser, Louis. "Ideology and Ideological State Apparatuses (Notes toward an Investigation)." In *Mapping Ideology*, ed. Slavoj Zizek, 100–40. New York: Verso Press, 1994.

Appel, Stephen. *Psychoanalysis and Pedagogy.* New York: Bergin and Garvey, 1999.

Austin, J. L. *How to Do Things with Words.* Cambridge: Harvard University Press, 1975.

Benjamin, Jessica. *The Bonds of Love: Psychoanalysis, Feminism, and the Problem of Domination.* New York: Pantheon, 1988.

———. *Like Subjects, Love Objects: Essays on Recognition and Social Difference.* New Haven: Yale University Press, 1995.

———. *Shadow of the Other: Intersubjectivity and Gender in Psychoanalysis.* New York: Routledge, 1998.

Benne, Kenneth. 1986. "The Locus of Educational Authority in Today's World." *Teachers College Record* 88, 1 (Fall 1986): 15–21.

Bingham, Charles. "What Friedrich Nietzsche Cannot Stand About Education: Toward a Pedagogy of Self-Reformulation." *Educational Theory* 51, 3 (2001).

———. "I Am the Missing Pages of the Text I Teach: Gadamer and Derrida on Teacher Authority." *Philosophy of Education 2001*, 265–72.

———. *Schools of Recognition: Identity Practices and Classroom Practices.* Boulder: Rowman and Littlefield, 2001.

———. "Who are the Philosophers of Education?" *Studies in Philosophy and Education* 24, 1 (2005).

Britzman, Deborah. *Lost Subjects, Contested Objects: Toward a Psychoanalytic Inquiry of Learning.* Albany: State University of New York Press, 1999.

Deleuze, Gilles. *Nietzsche and Philosophy.* Trans. Hugh Tomlinson. New York: Columbia University Press, 1983.

Derrida, Jacques. "Before the Law." In *Acts of Literature*, ed. Derek Attridge. New York: Routledge, 1992.

———. *Of Grammatology.* Trans. Gayatri Chakravorty Spivak. Baltimore: The Johns Hopkins University Press, 1974.

Dewey, John. "Authority and Social Change." In *Authority and the Individual.* Cambridge: Harvard University Press, 1937.

———. *Experience and Education.* New York: Collier Books, 1963.

———. *The Child and Curriculum.* Chicago: University of Chicago Press, 1990.

Egan, Kieran. *The Educated Mind: How Cognitive Tools Shape Our Understanding.* Chicago: University of Chicago Press, 1997.

Fanon, Franz. *Black Skins/White Masks.* Trans. Charles Lam Markmann. New York: Grove Press, 1967.

Felman, Shoshana. *Jacques Lacan and the Adventure of Insight: Psychoanalysis in Contemporary Culture.* Cambridge: Harvard University Press, 1987.

Foucault, Michel. *The Order of Things: An Archaeology of the Human Sciences.* New York: Pantheon, 1971.

———. *Discipline and Punish: The Birth of the Prison.* New York: Pantheon, 1977.

———. *History of Sexuality I: An Introduction.* New York: Pantheon, 1978.

———. *Power/Knowledge: Selected Interviews and Other Writings 1972–1977.* New York: Pantheon, 1980.

———. *The Foucault Reader.* Ed. Paul Rabinow. New York: Pantheon Books, 1984.

———. *Technologies of the Self: A Seminar with Michel Foucault.* Ed. Luther H. Martin, Huck Gutman, and Patrick H. Hutton. Amherst: University of Massachusetts Press, 1988.

———. *The Use of Pleasure: The History of Sexuality, Volume 2.* Trans. Robert Hurley. New York: Vintage Books, 1990.

———. "What Is Enlightenment?" in *Michel Foucault: Ethics, Subjectivity and Truth*, ed. Paul Rabinow. New York: The New Press, 1997.

Freedman, Maurice. *The Confirmation of Otherness: In Family, Community, and Society.* New York: Pilgrim Press, 1973.

Freire, Paulo. *Pedagogy of the Oppressed.* New York: Continuum, 1970.

Fugard, Athol. *My Children! My Africa!* New York: Theatre Communications Group, 1989.

Gadamer, Hans-Georg. *Philosophical Hermeneutics.* Berkeley: University of California Press, 1976.

———. *Truth and Method.* New York: Continuum, 1994.

———. *The Enigma of Health.* London: Polity Press, 1996.

Giroux, Henry. "Authority, Intellectuals, and the Politics of Practical Learning." *Teachers College Record* 88, 1 (Fall 1986): 22–40.

———. *Pedagogy and the Politics of Hope.* Boulder: Westview, 1997.

———. *Schooling and the Struggle for Public Life.* Minneapolis: University of Minnesota Press, 1998.

Hadot, Pierre. *Philosophy as a Way of Life.* Ed. Arnold Davidson. Cambridge: Blackwell, 1995.

Haney, Kathleen M. *Intersubjectivity Revisited: Phenomenology and the Other.* Athens: Ohio University Press, 1994.

Hansen, David. "Well-Formed, Not Well-Filled: Montaigne and the Paths of Personhood." *Educational Theory* 52, 2 (Spring 2002).

Heidegger, Martin. "Letter on Humanism." In *Martin Heidegger: Basic Writings, Second Edition.* San Francisco: Harper, 1993.

Hirsch, E. D. *The Schools We Need and Why We Don't Have Them.* New York: Anchor Books, 1999.

Husserl, Edmund. *Cartesian Meditations.* Trans. Dorian Cairns. The Hague: Martinus Nijhoff, 1970.

Johnson, Barbara. "Using People: Kant with Winnicott." In *The Turn to Ethics,* ed. Marjorie Garber, Beatrice Hanssen, Rebecca L. Walkowitz, 47–63. New York: Routledge, 2000.

Kafka, Franz. *The Trial.* Trans. Willa and Edwin Muir. New York: Schocken, 1984.

———. *The Metamorphosis, In the Penal Colony, and Other Stories.* Trans. Willa and Edwin Muir. New York: Schocken, 1995.

———. *The Castle.* Trans. Mark Harman. New York: Schocken, 1998.

Kant, Immanuel. *Foundations of the Metaphysics of Morals.* New York: The Liberal Arts Press, 1959.

———. "What Is Enlightenment?" http://www.fordham.edu/halsall/mod/kant-whatis.html (Oct 2, 2005).

Lakoff, George, and Mark Taylor. *Metaphors We Live By.* Chicago: University of Chicago Press, 2003.

Laplance, Jean, and J. B. Pontalis. *The Language of Psycho-Analysis.* New York: W.W. Norton, 1974.

Lingis, Alphonso. *The Community of Those Who Have Nothing in Common.* Indianapolis: University of Indiana Press, 1994.

Mayo, Chris. "The Uses of Foucault" *Educational Theory* 50, 1 (2000): 103–16.

Merleau-Ponty, Maurice. *Phenomenology, Language and Sociology: Selected Essays of Maurice Merleau-Ponty.* Ed. John O'Neill. London: Heinemann, 1974.

de Montaigne, Michel. "On the Education of Children." In *Selected Essays,* ed. Blanchard Bates. New York: The Modern Library, 1949.

Morrison, Toni. *Playing in the Dark: Whiteness and the Literary Imagination.* New York: Vintage, 1993.

Nehemas, Alexander. *The Art of Living.* Berkeley: University of California Press, 1998.

Nietzsche, Friedrich. *Beyond Good and Evil.* Trans. Walter Kaufman. New York: Vintage Books, 1966.

———. *On the Genealogy of Morals.* Trans. Walter Kaufmann. New York: Vintage Books, 1967.

———. *The Gay Science.* Trans. Walter Kaufmann. New York: Vintage Books, 1974.

———. *Ecce Homo.* Trans. Walter Kaufman. New York: Vintage Books, 1989.

———. "Schopenhauer as Educator." In *Unfashionable Observations,* ed. Ernst Behler, 171–225. Stanford: Stanford University Press, 1995.

Plato. *Meno.* Trans. G. M. A. Grube. Indianapolis: Hackett, 1976.

———. *The Last Days of Socrates: Euthyphro; The Apology; Creto; Phaedo.* New York: Penguin Classics, 1993.

Rajchman, John. *Michel Foucault: The Freedom of Philosophy.* New York: Columbia University Press, 1986.

Ravitch, Diane. *The Schools We Deserve*. New York: Basic Books, 1985.

Robertson, Emily. "Teacher Authority and Teaching for Liberation." *Philosophy of Education Society 1994* <http://www.ed.uiuc.edu/eps/pes~yearbook/94_docs/roberso.htm> (June 10, 2000).

Rorty, Richard. *The Consequences of Pragmatism*. Minneapolis: University of Minnesota Press, 1982.

Sankowski, Edward. "Autonomy, Education and Politics." *Philosophy of Education Society* <http://www.ed.uiuc.edu/eps/pes~yearbook/1998/sankowski.html> (July 15, 2000).

Santner, Eric L. *On the Psychotheology of Everyday Life: Reflections on Freud and Rosenweig*. Chicago: University of Chicago Press, 2001.

Shor, Ira. *Empowering Education : Critical Teaching for Social Change*. Chicago: University of Chicago Press, 1992.

———. *Critical Teaching and Everyday Life*. Chicago: University of Chicago Press, 1987.

Stewart, John. *Language as Articulate Contact: Towards a Post-Semiotic Philosophy of Language*. Albany: State University of New York Press, 1995.

Stewart, John, ed., *Beyond the Symbol Model*. Albany: State University of New York Press, 1996.

White, Patricia. 1986. "Self-respect, Self-esteem, and the School: A Democratic Perspective on Authority." *Teachers College Record* 88, 1 (Fall 1986): 95–106.

Winnicott, D. W. *Playing and Reality*. New York: Routledge, 1971.

Index

absence, 65ff
agency, 3, 12ff, 67ff, 80, 82ff, 91ff, 130ff
Althusser, Louis, 10, 153*n*
amor fati, 102
anamnesis, 44
Appel, Stephen, 161*n*
Austin, J.L., 27, 59, 61, 154*n*, 155*n*
authority
  and absence, 65ff, 146–147
  arguments based on, 134
  and authoritarianism, 19ff, 35, 38, 111, 119, 128, 132, 136, 137, 149
  and authoritativeness, 19ff, 35, 38, 45ff, 50, 52, 53, 69, 72, 73, 78, 83
  authority-versus-freedom dilemma, 134–136
  and balance, 142–145
  the circuit of, 6, 7, 37, 38, 67, 69, 125–128, 137ff
  its content, form, and authorship 47–48
  of culture, 105–107
  and epistemology, 107–109
  as force without significance, 41–45
  and hermeneutics, 19–22, 113ff
  of knowledge, 107–109
  and language, 54–63
  and literature, 41–53, 61–63, 150–151
  and maturity, 7–8

  monological, 7–9
  of nature, 104–105
  and presence, 66ff
  and political action, 31–39
  and the psyche, 67ff, 136ff
  and questioning, 111ff
  and the spoken word, 9ff, 74ff, 149–150
  and supplementarity, 22–27
  and texts, 17ff
  as a thing or substance, 2ff, 31, 45, 52, 53, 58, 152
  types of: traditional, progressive, and critical: 3–4, 28ff
  use of, 87ff
autonomy, 3, 21, 55, 67, 89, 90, 91, 92, 142

banking education, 130ff
"Before the Law" (Kafka), 41ff
Benjamin, Jessica, 67ff, 79ff, 137–139, 155*n*, 156*n*, 161*n*, 162*n*
Benne, Kenneth, 155*n*
Bingham, Charles, 154*n*, 159*n*, 162*n*
Black Skins/White Masks (Fanon), 11
Britzman, Deborah, 161*n*
Buber, Martin
  I-It relationship and, 139
  I-Thou relationship and, 139

capacity, 14, 15, 83, 102, 105, 107, 108, 129, 133, 134
Cartesian Meditations (Husserl), 76

170 Index

communication

and the sender-receiver model, 54ff

and performativity, 58ff

communities of difference, 55

critical perspectives on authority,
3–4, 24ff, 112, 125

culture, 105–107

curriculum, 21, 22, 26, 27, 39, 47ff,
62, 123, 131, 141, 142

Deleuze, Gilles, 117, 160n

Derrida, Jacques, 19, 22ff, 38, 39,
41ff, 154n, 155n

Dewey, John, 73, 88, 94, 124, 133,
155n, 156n, 157n, 160n, 161n

dialogue, 8, 75, 79, 82ff, 115, 117,
118, 123, 124, 134, 144, 150

domination and submission, 15,
70–74, 78, 79, 130, 137ff

Egan, Kieran, 98, 158n

elenchus, 54

enlightenment, 7, 8, 9, 13, 14, 20,
21, 55, 57, 89, 133, 135, 136

empowerment, 21, 43, 94ff, 123,
132, 133

epistemology, 107–109

Fanon, Franz, 11, 12, 136, 153n

fantasy, 70, 138, 139, 140, 141,
142, 145

Felman, Shoshana, 161n

forgetfulness, 103–104

Foucault, Michel, 13–15, 90–91, 98,
99, 106–109, 153n, 157n, 162n

Freedman, Maurice, 162n

freedom, 4, 8, 9, 12, 13, 14, 20, 21,
88, 107, 129ff

Freire, Paulo, 8, 9, 128ff, 153n,
160n, 161n, 162n, 163n

Fugard, Athol, 32–38, 154n

Gadamer, Hans-Georg, 19–22, 25–
27, 113ff, 153n, 154n, 155n,
160n

Giroux, Henry, 153n, 155n

good enough mother, 93–97

good enough teacher, 93–97

grades, 43, 82

Hadot, Pierre, 159n

Haney, Kathleen M., 156n

Hansen, David, 159n

Heidegger, Martin, 117, 160n

hermeneutics, 19ff, 113ff

Hirsch, E.D, 153n

Husserl, Edmund, 76, 77, 79, 156n

Ideology and Ideological State
Apparatuses (Althusser), 10

Ideology, 10, 29, 30, 47, 131, 133,
137, 143

interpellation, 10

intersubjectivity, 76ff, 87ff, 97, 139

intrapsychic, 69, 79ff, 138ff

Johnson, Barbara, 157n

Kafka, Franz, 41ff, 154n

Kafkaesque, 42, 43

Kant, Immanuel, 7–9, 55ff, 88ff,
133, 153n, 157n, 162n

knowledge, 107–109

Lakoff, George, 54, 155n

literature, 41–53, 61–63

its content, form, and authorship,
45–47

its framing and referentiality, 46ff

language theory, 53ff, 113ff

Laplance, Jean, 155n

Liberalism, 56, 129, 130, 133ff,
140, 142, 143

Lingis, Alphonso, 55, 56, 155n

linguistic turn, 116

literary relation, 41ff

and the teacher, 51ff

and the student, 48ff

maturity (and Enlightenment), 7, 55,
58

Mayo, Chris, 160n

Meno (Plato), 43, 44

Merleau-Ponty, Maurice, 75, 77, 79,
80, 156n

de Montaigne, Michel, 108, 159n
morality, 88ff
Morrison, Toni, 26, 27, 154n
My Children! My Africa! (Fugard), 32ff

nature, faced with the authority of,
    104–105
Nehemas, Alexander, 99, 104, 157n,
    158n, 159n
Nietzsche, Friedrich, 89, 90, 92, 98ff,
    108, 109, 157n, 158n, 159in

object relations theory, 67–70,
    80–82, 89, 91ff, 137–139
objectification, 80, 140, 141
oppressed, 130, 132, 135, 138
oppressor, 130, 134, 138, 139

pairing, 76, 77
Pedagogy of the Oppressed (Freire),
    128ff.
performativity, 58–63
Plato, 98, 123, 124, 150, 151, 154n
Playing in the Dark: Whiteness and
    the Literary Imagination
    (Morrison), 26
Pontalis, J. B., 155n
power, 2, 3, 13, 14, 19, 20, 21, 27,
    90, 91
pragmatism, 88
pragmatic intersubjectivity, 88ff
presence, 65ff
problem-posing education, 134–136
progressivism, 3–4, 7, 8, 13, 18, 25,
    28ff, 39, 47, 51, 94, 111, 112,
    124, 125, 133, 149, 150
psychoanalysis
    and absence, 67ff
    and Paulo Freire, 136ff
    and intersubjectivity, 69, 79ff,
        139–140
    and intrapsychic life, 69, 79ff,
        138ff
    and language, 79ff

questioning, 111ff
    and circuitry, 125–128, 145–146
    and throwing dice, 117–118, 126

false, 114–120
    and hidden statements, 113–114
    and steering, 116, 119, 120, 122
    and non-superficiality, 122–123
    true, 114–127
    and ventriloquism, 121
    and responding with a question,
        125–128

Rabinow, Paul, 153n
Rajchman, John, 159n
Ravitch, Diane, 153n
Robertson, Emily, 155n
Rorty, Richard, 157n
recognition, 67ff, 79ff, 137ff, 162n
rational communities, 55ff
reciprocity, 8, 15, 146
relation
    authority as, 2ff
    and balance, 142–145
    between self and culture, 105–107
    between self and nature, 104–105
    between self and knowledge,
        107–109
    with absent others, 65ff
    and questioning, 111ff
remnant, 69ff
Rorty, Richard, 157n

Sankowski, Edward, 155n
Santner, Eric L., 61, 62, 154n, 155n
self-fashioning, 97ff
sender-receiver model of language,
    54ff
Shor, Ira, 153n, 161n
signified and signifier, 120ff
Socratic Method, 43–44, 111–112,
    123–124, 159n
speech, 9ff, 74ff, 149–150
spoken and written word, 9ff, 74ff,
    149–150
Stewart, John, 54, 155n
submission (and domination), 15,
    70–74, 78, 79, 130, 137ff
supplementarity, 22ff
    and progressivism, 29
    and traditionalism, 29
    and criticalism, 29–30

Taylor, Mark, 54, 155*n*
traditionalism, 3–4, 28ff, 34, 98,
　　112, 125
Truth and Method (Gadamer), 122, 123

using others, 87ff

"What is Enlightenment?" (Kant), 7,
　　89, 133, 162*n*
"What is Enlightenment?" (Foucault),
　　162*n*
White, Patricia, 155*n*
Winnicott, D.W., 89, 91ff, 157*n*